A
Pictorial Guide
to Biblical
Archaeology

Dedicated

to my wife

PEGGY

Faithful Companion and Co-laborer

in the Gospel

A
Pictorial Guide
to Biblical
Archaeology

Robert T. Boyd

Introduction by Charles F. Pfeiffer

HARVEST HOUSE PUBLISHERS
Eugene, Oregon 97402

ACKNOWLEDGMENT

Acknowledgment is gratefully made to Dr. Joseph P. Free, professional archaeologist and Director of the Near East School of Archaeology and Biblical Studies on the Mount of Olives in Jerusalem, who not only stirred my interest in Biblical archaeology but gave me the privilege of being a staff member one season with the Wheaton College Archaeological Expedition at the Old Testament site of Dothan in northern Palestine, and to Dr. Charles F. Pfeiffer, professor of Ancient Literatures at Central Michigan University, Mount Pleasant, Michigan, whose encouragement contributed greatly to the publication of this book.

PHOTOLITHOPRINTED BY CUSHING - MALLOY, INC.
ANN ARBOR, MICHIGAN, UNITED STATES OF AMERICA

Introduction

Biblical archaeology continues to interest the man on the street as well as the pastor and scholar. Who has not heard of the Dead Sea Scrolls? The romance of accidental discoveries in exotic lands revives our childhood fantasies of high adventure. These are true stories, and they come from lands with which we are familiar from our books of ancient history — and, more important, from our Bible.

Archaeology and history are closely interrelated. Archaeology, in fact, provides the material from which books of ancient history are made. Western civilization never quite forgot the glories of Athens and Rome. As a result ancient history meant, until a few decades ago, the study of the lives and deeds of Greek and Roman worthies. College courses in ancient history often devoted one semester to Greece, and a second to Rome. As records from Egypt, Sumer, Assyria, Babylonia, the land of the Hittites, and other peoples of the ancient Near East became known, a chapter or two of preliminary material was tacked on to the volume on Greece. Herodotus was still "the father of History," although that eminent Greek freely acknowledged his debt to Egyptian and other sources. Archaeology, however, helps us push the pages of history back many centuries prior to the days of Herodotus.

Many graduates from our best universities are woefully ignorant of the revolution in our understanding of the past which archaeology has brought about. Simply as a matter of general education, any informed person should read widely in the literature of archaeology. Knowing our past provides a perspective for studying our present, and our future.

The Christian has more than an academic interest in ancient history, and in the light archaeology throws on Biblical events. His faith is historically oriented. He declares faith in a Savior who was born when Caesar Augustus was Emperor of the Roman Empire, and when Herod the Great was king of the Jews. His historic creeds affirm that Jesus "suffered under Pontius Pilate." While much that the Christian affirms cannot, in its very nature, be verified as historical data, the basic outlines of Old and New Testament events are placed in a historic context. Archaeology helps us to see the events in that context, and to understand the Bible as a book dealing with actual history. Too often have we accepted the child's definition of faith: "Believing things you know aren't so." Our faith may precede our knowledge of history and archaeology, but our faith cannot survive if it runs counter to our understanding of the events of history and archaeological data.

The Christian may think it is the purpose of archaeology to prove the Bible true. Such an affirmation fails to do justice to the Bible as a book which bears its own claim to man's faith and devotion. It also assumes that the archaeologist approaches his subject with a closed mind, as if to say that he is interested only in that which "confirms" the Biblical data. No honest archaeologist could accept such an assignment. Like every true scientist, he is seeking knowledge. Ideas held earlier may be confirmed, or it may be necessary to correct them in the light of newer discoveries. Humility is, of course, always necessary. The Bible may be misinterpreted by exegetes with insufficient data from which to make a valid judgment. Archaeologists may draw hasty conclusions on the basis of insufficient evidence. We make no claim for infallibility for either the Biblical scholar or the archaeologist. We insist, however, that the more we know of our Bible — and of historical and archaeological data — the less apt we are to make serious errors of judgment and interpretation.

The archaeological mind must be objective, rather than subjective. Christianity has both objective and subjective elements. The act of commitment to Jesus Christ is personal, and unverifiable save through the fruit of the Spirit evident in the committed life. If we could handle the bones of Paul (and we can't) there would still be no objective evidence that he was a Christian. His career, documented in the New Testament, is all the evidence we need. Yet we must not draw from this fact the thought that verifiable historicity is unnecessary.

The Christian affirms that God was in Christ reconciling the world to Himself. The Word became flesh and dwelt among us. Men saw His glory. He suffered and, at a point of history, died. On Easter morning the tomb was empty. If these are not facts, then Christianity has no factual basis and should, in all honesty, be abandoned. The apostle Paul was bold enough to say, "If Christ has not been raised, your faith is futile, and you are still in your sins" (I Cor. 15:17).

The Old Testament, like the New, has a historical base. Men such as Nebuchadnezzar and Cyrus are well known on the pages of secular history. Sennacherib's annals tell of his siege of Jerusalem. The Bible is an important source for a study of ancient history, and the study of history helps us to understand the uniqueness of Israel among the peoples of the Fertile Crescent.

This book, written by a pastor and evangelist, aims to present the results of a century of archaeological work in clear, understandable form. Hopefully it will introduce the lay worker to the fascination of archaeological research, and demonstrate its relevance to Christian faith.

—Charles F. Pfeiffer

Mount Pleasant, Michigan
May 24, 1969

List of Illustrations

Contents

The Romance of Archaeology

The subject of Archaeology, especially as it relates to God's Word, *can* be made interesting. Technical terms and expressions often cause the average person to become disinterested in any subject where an "interpreter" must assist. For years archaeology was as "dead" to me as its name implied, not because it was not an interesting subject, but because of my becoming bogged down in so much subject matter. While subject matter is necessary and important to any subject or science, I personally feel there is a need for a book in archaeology that all can understand, whether he be layman, Bible teacher, Sunday School teacher, student or minister. The need is for a book the reader may grasp without losing interest before he reaches the end of the first chapter.

Artifacts which have been resurrected from the tells and tombs of the Bible lands by the pick and spade of the archaeologist have given us living messages from a buried past. Our Western minds, ignorant of Biblical customs, which are Eastern, find archaeology helpful in illuminating portions of Scripture by providing abundant material to fill in the background, giving us better perspective. It helps also to correct mistaken concepts regarding Biblical history, which have raised a multitude of questions in the minds of believers seeking a better understanding of the Word of God. Things which are not understood are "dead," but a simple explanation can often make a subject come alive.

This, then, is the purpose of this book — to make the subject of Archaeology so

1. A Cluster of Clay Tablets

2. *Tomb Interior*

interesting that those who believe the Bible will recognize its worth in the field of Christian evidences. With archaeological information at hand, the believer can use this "tool" in making the Word of God known to others. As the written Word begins to take on life, it reveals the Living Word, even Jesus Christ Himself, who is the theme of the Bible and who is God's answer to man's age-old problem — sin.

The author seeks to take the reader on his own archaeological expedition. Imagine the thrill of making your way to a buried city in the land of the Bible. It looks like a mound of dirt to others but to you it is a hidden past about to be resurrected. And *you* are going to find something that reveals life as it was centuries ago! You may unearth a number of clay tablets clustered together (*No. 1*), or other inscribed objects. You may even bring to light a clay tablet or an inscribed stone that pinpoints a person or an event mentioned in history. It may relate to the Bible itself. You may dis-

cover a tomb (*No. 2*) in which skeletons and personal belongings buried with the deceased unfold life in a given age. At this site (mound, or "tell"), you will find countless "potsherds" (broken pieces of pottery). A fairly large piece may have served as a dipper; smaller pieces may have been used to carry live coals of fire from one household to another. Among the thousands of potsherds unearthed at your "dig" (where the actual excavation is being conducted), you might discover an "ostracon" (an inscribed pottery fragment). Its text might reveal a receipt or a delivery bill for shipment of some commodity. Later, we will show how pottery tells "time" — giving the approximate date for such findings.

Each piece of broken pottery will remind you of Job, who found comfort in scraping his boils with a potsherd (2:8). Potsherds will remind you of man's being at enmity with God, without strength, and constantly at strife with his fellow-man (Ps. 22:15; Isa. 45:9). Every broken piece will also be a reminder of a sinner's heart — broken and completely beyond human repair, forgotten like a broken vessel (Prov. 26:23; Ps. 31:12). However, you may even find an unbroken object, and that will remind you of a vessel molded by the Potter, meet for the Master's use.

On our imaginary expedition you will not be satisfied until you have a "working knowledge" of what Archaeology really is. You will discover that here is evidence helpful in witnessing for Christ. Here is evidence which offers a vast amount of support to the Bible and its historical claims. If ever Christians needed such evidence as this, *it is now.* Also, while on this expedition, may the Spirit of God help you to "discover" evidence in your own life that could be used in revealing His "Living Message" of hope to a lost and dying world.

Bob Boyd

Definitions

An *ARCHAEOLOGIST* is a student of history whose career leads to ruins.

ARCHAEOLOGY is a scientific study of the remains of population centers, written materials, artifacts and monuments of the past, both historic and pre-historic. It simply means an investigation of ancient things which were lost but are now found. Archaeology does not seek to prove anything — it just works with facts — the evidence at hand.

An *ARTIFACT* is anything discovered that has been made by human skill. Artifacts are commonly called *OBJECTS.*

A *BAULK* is the untouched section of an excavation about three feet wide, left at regular intervals to serve as steps to the lower levels as the digging proceeds. Baulks provide a view of the levels in profile while holding tags and pegs necessary for surveying levels and recording finds.

BIBLICAL ARCHAEOLOGY. From a Christian viewpoint, the aim of archaeology is to learn everything possible about life and lands in Biblical times. It is interested in geography, for history has its roots in the soil. It reveals how natural barriers protected nations, or became sources of disunity and isolation, what bearing natural resources (water, pasture land, ore, climate) or the lack of them had upon people, and how livelihood was affected by distance from or nearness to trade routes on land and sea. It supports the historical claims of God's own people and of nations and kingdoms related to Israel's past. Its findings confirm passages of Scripture and illuminate numerous Biblical customs.

CIVILIZATION. Until man began to live in settled communities, there was little opportunity for him to solve the problems of his environment. Civilization is basically the sum of man's

15

answers at any given stage to such questions of society.

CUNEIFORM is the ancient Mesopotamian "wedge-shaped" style of writing, made by pressing a stylus in soft clay, or by chiseling in stone.

A DIG is a familiar term used for an excavation.

EPIGRAPH. Writing on a wall, statue, or other surface.

An EXCAVATION is the scientific uncovery of past civilization at a given site.

An EXPEDITION is an organized team of skilled experts and assistants on a specific project.

IN-SITU is the actual location in which an artifact is discovered.

An OCCUPATIONAL LEVEL is a single level in a tell, or the level of the city at any given time during its existence. Levels are also called STRATA (levels of stratification).

An OSTRACON is a pottery fragment upon which a message has been inscribed in ink. OSTRACA (plural).

POTSHERD, or SHERD. A piece of broken pottery.

A SITE is the location of the excavation.

SURFACE SOIL is the top soil of the mound.

A TELL is the site to be excavated — an artificial MOUND or hill formed by successive layers of human occupation, resulting from garbage and trash disposal, the ruins of old buildings and city walls and accumulated dust or sand. The highest layer or level of occupation is the most recent and the lowest is the oldest.

VIRGIN SOIL is the top soil of a natural hill upon which the first city was built. The archaeologist can tell when he "hits" virgin soil — he no longer can find any evidence of a buried civilization.

A STELE (or STELA) is an upright stone slab or monument bearing a sculptured design or an inscription.

CHAPTER 1

Once upon a Time

With all the advantages of our age — science, medicine, jet and space achievements — one would think the farther back the archaeologist went the more primitive he would find man to be. This, however, is not the case. Findings at excavations have proved a suddenness with which civilization appeared in the world. Pre-historic civilization shows man building houses, palaces, temples and cities. Archaeologists have expressed surprise and astonishment at the high rate of culture in the very earliest stages of the Egyptians. It is possible today to reconstruct in remarkable detail the ritual worship of early man, all about life in the courts of ancient monarchs and their kingdoms, what the average "Joe" did for a living, and what schoolboys at Ur of the Chaldees were taught before the days of Abraham.

Everything found by the archaeologist in ancient tombs or buried cities means *something*. Events and names which are recorded on clay tablets or inscribed on stone are not *just* names and places. They total up the daily events in the lives of human beings who lived centuries ago. Those who left these records were just plain, ordinary, common folks. These people *lived*. They had hopes and ambitions which caused them to forge ahead. They were red-blooded men and women who laughed and cried, who enjoyed pleasures and endured pain and sorrow, who hungered and thirsted, loved and hated, worked and played. Their life was as important to them as ours is to us.

How surprising this must be to the proponents of the theory of evolution! True, many crude objects have been discovered which are "primitive" to our way of thinking; but the archaeologist is *not* finding evidence supporting the theory that the more ancient the period and people, the less "advanced" they were. As the archaeologist has worked back he has *not* found traces of civilization ceasing altogether and "ape man" appearing, nor has he found skeletons or skeletal patterns which reveal changes from one stage to another. Every pre-historic skeleton of man discovered thus far *is* completely human. Each one has been within the range of the physical variation of the modern human race. Man is man, and archaeology is demonstrating that no matter how far back we go, man *is* civilized.

EARLY CIVILIZATION

The Bible itself speaks of early man as a civilized being. Adam was intelligent, able to name animals and to have dominion over every living thing (Gen. 1:28; 2:20). Acquainted with a knowledge of husbandry, he became an agriculturist and from the earth he ate the herb of the field and in the sweat of his face he ate bread (Gen. 3:18). Abel's sacrifice to the Lord suggests that he was an herdsman, while Cain's suggests that he was a farmer (Gen. 4:3, 4). Cain also built a city, revealing his architectural, carpentry and masonry ability. Many excavations in ancient Mesopotamia show early village and city life. Some cities

3. Houses and Walls

assumed a splendor from towering temples. The dwellings built in the temple areas were small, one-story houses built of mud, sun-dried bricks or stones. Some of the bricks measured 21 x 15 x 5½ inches. Today houses in remote Bible lands are built the same way (*No. 3*) and much of the life of the present-day inhabitants is patterned after that of their ancient ancestors.

BUILDING

At ancient Kish the pillars, walls and steps of a once beautiful "kingdom"

4. Kingdom Palace at Kish

palace were discovered (*No. 4*). The extensive ruins indicate that its king was very cultured and wealthy. Items found were artistic, and the pillars and walls were richly decorated with varied animal figures. One archaeological feature was the true arch. Also found in this city were pieces of painted jars, flint implements (such as hand axes, saws and cutting knives), copper mirrors, various farm tools, bone fishhooks, baked bricks with inscriptions, a man's bust (*No. 5*), chariot wheels (*No. 6*), geometric patterns, and everyday household items such as bowls, jars and lamps. From Nippur, the religious and scientific center of ancient Babylon, has come a city map (*No. 7*), showing locations of city walls, temples, gates, canals and government buildings.

POTTERY

Pottery was man's first invention, and pottery making certainly became his leading industry. Bowls, vases, jars, lamps,

5. *Early Man*

6. *Chariot Wheels at Kish*

7. *Map of City of Nippur*

8. *Ancient Egyptian Potter.*

etc., were crudely fashioned by hand (No. 24). Later came the potter's wheel, which was usually turned by the potter himself as he shaped the soft clay. *No. 8* depicts an ancient potter shaping a bowl with three newly made jars by his side. "Mass" production came when the small wheel was placed on a larger one. Turned by a helper, this enabled the potter to use both hands in fashioning his pottery. The potter's "wheels" are alluded to by Jeremiah (18:3). The foot-tread appeared on the potter's wheel a few centuries before Christ, and is a common sight in the Holy Land today.

The process of preparing clay was simple. Clean clay was chosen. Treading to remove air bubbles and a proper amount of water brought about a consistent texture. The ancient potter set the pattern for many of our household utensils, such as cooking pots, casseroles and kettles. Pottery vats took the place of storage bins, boxes and bags. Our dinner-ware designs today appear to be but "hand-me-downs" from early man. Children's toys — including dolls, dishes, animals — were pottery. The "army canteen" was first made of clay. A method was devised in baking or firing the flask (cruse) so that the water would be cooled by evaporation through the walls of the vessel. Nomads make use of this type vessel today. The ancient Babylonians developed the art of pottery to where it was even used to make sickles.

BUSINESS

Early civilized man was businesslike. Jabel (Gen. 4:20) saw the value of animal husbandry measured in terms of oxen, sheep, cattle and hides. Cain the builder knew, no doubt, how to barter for needed materials. Those whose livelihood was gained from the soil used grain and cooking utensils as units of price. Cave dwellers who made more flint objects than needed found those who were anxious to swap necklaces, shells, and headdresses for flint knives, etc. Villages produced merchants whose wares were supplied to desert folks. Some "city slickers" became "traveling salesmen," who distributed not only their goods, but their language, system of writing, and arts.

Nothing proves better the intellectual and business ability of early man than his business records. They show that recessions and depressions were practically unknown. The ancient Assyrians devised the first drafts or checks — clay tablets which stated what each was worth in silver. One tablet was a receipt of interest at the rate of 20 per cent which had been paid on a loan of four shekels of silver for a period of six months. Another tablet had to do with a loan involving a sixty-year lease, with terms having been met in advance. There are records of deeds, mortgages, the sale of slaves, bankruptcy proceedings, of the purchasing of lots and houses, the sale of a silver mine, wills, promissory notes, and the registry of ships as they docked at various ports to discharge passengers and unload goods. Fragments of clay which served as stamps tell us of a postal system between Canaan and Babylonia, and other records reveal a land-trade route that extended from the Mediterranean to Babylon.

WRITING

Writing became an early art. Probably the first form of writing was painted pictures and symbols. Then man invented the "printing press" — a "cylinder seal" (*No. 9*). Symbols used to identify cities, gods, persons and events (their god battling a foe or a hunting scene)

9. *Cylinder Seals and Impressions*

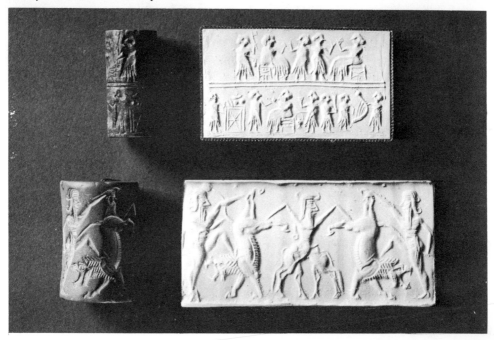

10. *Pictorial Clay Tablet*   11. *Pictorial Symbols with Cuneiform*

were carved on small rollers or cylinders made of alabaster stone, or jadite, or were fashioned out of wet clay and then hardened. The cylinder was then rolled over flattened, soft clay, and the picture story was "printed" or recorded. It was soon learned that these symbols served the same purpose when impressed on clay, and this led to the tablet. A bone or reed stylus was used to make the impressions. The pictorial tablet (*No. 10*) is a sample of man's earliest "writing." Although it has not yet been deciphered, these pictorial symbols were clearly impressed.

Someone has suggested that since early writing was in the form of marks, or symbols, writing began when God put a "mark" on Cain after he had slain Abel (Gen. 4:15). Nobody knows what the mark was, but it was distinguishable. Although Cain suffered punishment, God's mercy, in the form of a "mark" or "sign," protected him from the same fate of his brother.

As the scribes progressed, expressions in marks became expressions in words. Afterwards, certain words were put together, forming sentences, and full-

fledged "writing" appeared. Picture *No. 11* is a clay tablet with both the pictorial symbol and ancient Mesopotamian cuneiform. In this wedge-shaped style over six hundred signs were used representing both syllables and ideas. Together with the use of such symbols as plants, animals, birds, fish, and everyday implements in writing and reading, they served as steps in scientific approaches to zoology, agriculture, and botany. Botanical terms of our day, such as cumin, myrrh, chickory and hyssop, all come from Mesopotamia. Astronomy and mathematics were well-known sciences.

The Egyptians were also making "headlines" in the art of writing. Their style is known as "hieroglyphics" (*No. 12*). Pictured is one of the oldest mathematical documents ever unearthed. It contains eighty-five exercises in arithmetic and geometry, with their solutions. This mathematical document was written on papyrus and is still wonderfully preserved. Despite an awkward numerical system, the ancient Egyptians were able to multiply and divide, reduce fractions, calculate the areas of trapezoids, circles and triangles, and compute the volume of cylinders.

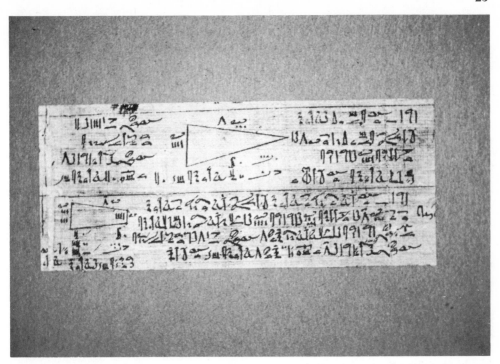

12. *Hieroglyphics*

13. *Clay Tablet and Envelope*

That writing became an art as well as a useful means of communication is shown by the "letter" (left) and the "envelope" (right) (*No. 13*). Even the envelope contained a part of the message. The "scarab" (*No. 14*) was man's way of putting his "John Henry" on the dotted line. It had the shape of a beetle. Its owner's insignia was carved on the underside. A string was inserted in a hole which had been bored lengthwise through the scarab, and it was worn around the neck. If property was sold, animals deposited at public stables, or any business matters transacted, it was inscribed on a soft clay tablet and the receipt was "signed" by pressing the scarab on the clay.

Of the many contributions which Mesopotamia has given to civilization none compares in importance to that which has been achieved as a result of the introduction of writing. From these people has come what we call the "sexagesimal system," which divides the circle into 360°, the hour into sixty minutes and the minute into sixty seconds. In addition to volumes of subjects already mentioned, there have been unearthed dictionaries, archives of kings, lexicons, encyclopedias, grammars, commentaries, and complete works on religion, law, medicine and science. One record tells of a god who became the Babylonian Noah. Having hid some sacred writings before the flood, he later dug them up after the flood. One ancient Mesopotamian king loved to read accounts of the time *before* the great flood. The post-flood records found at Ur (Abraham's hometown) show that children were taught the three "R's" — readin', 'ritin' and 'rithmetic. One tablet contained a multiplication table of nine (9 x 1 to 9 x 50). Also included in their curriculum was geography, as indicated by the "World Map" (*No. 15*). This map shows Babylon at the center on the river Euphrates, surrounded by oceans, distant mountainous districts and swamps. It

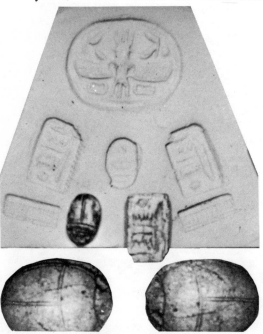

14. *Scarabs and Impressions*

15. *World Map*

was drawn in 2300 B.C. by Sargon of Agade to illustrate his campaigns. This king penetrated Asia Minor, and his exploits, mentioned in the preceding text, were well known throughout Asia eight hundred years later. It is hard to believe, but students were wrestling with ancient history 3500 years ago!

GOVERNMENT

Various forms of government can be pieced together by records from clay tablets left by the Mesopotamians or by the writings on papyrus left by the Egyptians. In seeking to answer society's problems, many laws were enacted. Law was accorded a place of honor and prominence in the culture structure of our distant ancestors. Legal codes guided the ruler and safeguarded the citizens. We call this democracy today. Even though a king became the mighty ruler of an empire, he was still a servant of the law and not its source. He obeyed the god who gave the laws, which amounted to a divine guarantee of the individual's rights. These laws had "foundations as firm as heaven and earth."

King Hammurabi of Babylon is shown (*No. 16*) receiving laws from the sun-god Shamash, the god of Justice. As Hammurabi stands before Shamash, he receives, as an act of worship, a ring and a rod, and in turn, Hammurabi attributes to Shamash the inspiration he received to gather laws of justice into a code. He then represents himself as the embodiment of justice. The whole code consisted of about 282 laws, which dealt with three classes of citizens — the upper-class free man, the middle-class free man, and the slave. Fees and wages were regulated for professional men, for the "white collar" worker, and for the slaves. One law dealt with marriage. As the father received payment for his daughter, he "gave" his daughter away by pressing

16. Hammurabi and Shamash

his scarab to the legal document or marriage license. Watching eagerly nearby, the happy couple stood ready to say "I do." There were laws which related to property rights, rights of children, and divorce. Taxes were imposed, and payment was due periodically. When new taxes were levied, a memorandum of this edict was inscribed, and promptly relayed by couriers to all the provinces of the kingdom.

Offenses, as well as the punishment for each crime, were listed in this code. Listed were sorcery, bearing false witness, theft and receiving stolen goods, stealing at a fire and highway robbery, faulty construction of a building which resulted in death, juvenile delinquency, adultery, murder and kidnapping — to name just a few. It mentioned three types of execution — burning, drowning, and impalement. Bodily mutilation was imposed for crimes not warranting death, such as branding the body by cutting off an ear, tongue, hand or breast, or blinding an eye. For a son who struck his father, his hand was severed. A physician suffered the same fate if he had to "bury his mistake." Punishment was on an "eye for an eye and a tooth for a tooth" basis. Although Hammurabi lived between the days of Abraham and Moses (his code was written *ca.* 1723 B.C.), and while there are some codes older by some three hundred years, these laws serve to illustrate the receiving and imposing of similar laws during the earlier period of man's history.

METALLURGY

The pick and spade of the archaeologist have uncovered evidence that metallurgy was developed in pre-historic days. The earliest mention of metals in the Bible is in reference to Tubal-cain — an "instructor skilled in every working method with copper and iron" (see Gen. 4: 22). Copper can be dated as early as 4500 B.C. With its introduction in the Stone Age, man's way of life changed completely, like ours from the horse and buggy days to the automobile.

Many scholars accept the book of Job as the oldest in the world, and in it is recorded the fact that metal is dug out of the earth (28:1, 2). Earliest known iron came from meteors and was known as "metal from heaven." Gold is mentioned in Genesis 2:11, 12; silver in Genesis 44:2; lead in Exodus 15:10; tin in Numbers 31:22, and iron in Numbers 35:16. Dross was freed from the metals by fire (Ezek. 22:17-22). Clay was used for molding hot metal (I Kings 7:46).

It is difficult to "date" the introduction of iron because, unlike copper, it rusts and disappears. However, iron had its place in international commerce about the period of Moses. During Saul's reign (1025 B.C.), the Philistines were skilled blacksmiths and controlled the industry in Palestine (I Sam. 13:19-23). Blacksmiths were so valuable they were listed among those who were taken prisoners (II Kings 24:14). The comparative value of metal is noted in Isaiah 60:17 and by Daniel (2:31, 32). It had an extensive commercial value in Ezekiel's day (27:12). Although metal had an early beginning in man's history, it appears that weapons have taken precedence over useful tools. (It certainly has in our military build-up.)

WAR AND WEAPONS

Early man often settled arguments on the battlefield. The ancient city of Lagash gives evidence of material and written remains of a battle with its rival neighbor, the city-state of Umma. The king's chariot had the city's emblem of a lion-headed eagle sinking its claws into the backs of two lions. Chariots were drawn by wild asses, and foot soldiers wore heavy cloaks fastened only at the neck to allow freedom of movement while fighting.

Weapons consisted of sling stones, spears, and bows and arrows. Sling stones (*No. 17,* upper), weighing about three-quarters of a pound and two inches in diameter, were used by "slingers" (*No. 18,* upper and lower left. See II Kings 3:25). The bronze spear head (No. 17, lower) varied in size, 5 to 8 inches, and was attached to a long pole. Spears were carried by "spearmen" (Ps. 68:30). "Archers" or "bowmen" (Gen. 49:23; Jer. 4:29) used bows and arrows (No. 18). Their headgear consisted of helmets made of metal (*No. 19*) or of leather, depending upon rank in the army. A gold helmet was found at Ur, and is dated 2500 B.C. It gives us an idea of armor worn prior to this time. As war "progressed" the "War Department" invented the "engine of war" (*No. 20*), which hurled large stones and shot

17. *Sling Stones and Bronze Spear*

18. *"Slingers" and Bowmen*

19. *Gold Helmet*

arrows against city towers and walls (II Chron. 26:15; Ezek. 26:9). The "engine of war" was the forerunner of our modern-day tank.

HOMES AND FAMILY LIFE

At pre-historic villages such as Tepe Gawra and Kish, there have been found complex structures of temples, defense works and houses. Many of the streets were narrow, permitting only "one way" traffic. Most towns were small — consisting of quarters for sleeping only. All else, including cooking and the gathering of families and friends, was done outside. The houses or rooms were constructed so that a wall was formed to protect the citizens, and the entrance into the "city" led into an open court or yard. In larger cities, houses also contained "parlor, bedroom and sink."

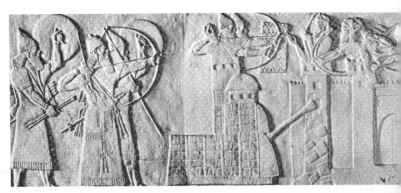

20. *Engine of War*

21. Woman Weaving

Women were "home-bodies." They cooked, worked in the fields, made clothes, etc. *No. 21* shows a wife weaving some material (possibly wool or linen), seated on a lion-footed stool, holding a spindle, and being fanned by a servant. The weights (*No. 22*) were used on looms to hold the wool or other material taut while weaving (left, Bronze Age weight, 3000 B.C., and a "manufactured" weight, 2000 B.C.). Stones were used to grind grain. The "saddle-quern" (*No. 23*) is similar to the "mill" referred to by Christ when He said, "Two women shall be grinding at the mill" (Matt. 24:41). The grinding base is 24 x 18 inches and the hand stone, which was used to rub over and crush the grain, is 18 inches long and weighs five pounds.

No. 24 shows four lamps with an age span of 2400 years. Number 1 is a crude hand-made lamp, 6 inches in diameter and 1½ inches deep (3000 B.C.). No.

22. Loom Weights

23. *Saddle Quern*

24. *Lamps*

2 is a lamp turned on a potter's wheel, having a "pinched" rim to secure the wick in place (2200 B.C.). No. 3 is a smaller lamp with a flat base and pinched rim (1600 B.C.). No. 4 is a small lamp on a stand, 3 inches high (900-600 B.C.).

Olives were crushed in an olive press (*No. 25*), and the juice or oil flowed into the small groove, then into the large opening where it was scooped up and poured into lamps for fuel or used in cooking.

Jewelry has been in vogue (probably) since the year 1! *No. 26* shows a mascara jar with spatula (top), a mirror (center, left), and rings and beads, which were the fashion of women. Men of the Near East also adorned themselves with jewelry. Bone and shell jewelry can be traced back as far as 8000 B.C. Common pieces of jewelry were gem seals, bracelets, ear and nose rings, anklets, pendants, and gold nets for the hair. Rebecca was presented with a gold earring and two bracelets (Gen. 24:22). When the Tabernacle was built the Israelites

25. *Olive Press*

26. *Jewelry*

27. *Crushed Skull*

28. *"Miss Ur"*

gave an offering of jewelry (Exod. 35:27). Job mentions precious stones used in jewelry (28:15-19).

Picture *No. 27* shows the crushed skull of a lady found in the Royal Tombs at Ur. "Madame X" is about 4400 years old. Her head was covered with gold leaves attached to bands of gold. A little below center are her teeth, and to the left are seen large gold earrings. Just beneath her teeth are fancy carved beads. *No. 28* is "Miss Ur" of 2500 B.C., showing the jewelry which was taken from the crushed skull. The gold was so finely beaten that it made handling difficult. Fancy jars and stone bottles were used for spices. Found at another site was a masterpiece — a spouted bowl made about 3000 B.C. from a single piece of volcanic glass. Not only was jewelry used by men, but barbering was also an art. Heads, as well as faces, were shaved "clean" by the barber who used a "straight" razor. Blades were made of sharp volcanic glass or flint and were "glued" to slate handles with bitumen.

MUSIC

Music has always been in the heart of man. We read of it in connection with Jubal (Gen. 4:21). Harps and lyres, with from three to ten strings, were found at Ur. At pre-historic Tepe Gawra archaeologists found the grave of a young boy, the right hand still clutching his instrument — playing pipes made of bone. The ram's horn was a popular instrument, and could have been the forerunner of the trumpet. Often mentioned in Scripture, it signaled war and peace, announced feast days, warned of danger, and was blown at the death of nobility. Wind instruments — flute and pipe — had a wide secular use, and were largely associated with sex orgies among the heathen. Mirth and song, with instruments, were a part of family life (Gen. 31:27). Israel used timbrels and singing to celebrate the drowning of Pharaoh in the Red Sea (Exod. 15:20, 21). Just before Moses ascended Mount Sinai, trumpets were played (Exod. 19:16). When David defeated the Philistines, instruments were played and the women danced and sang (*No. 29*). When Solomon was anointed king, wind instruments and trumpets "rent the earth" (I Kings 1:39, 40). Psalm 150 is praise to God on many instruments (trumpets, timbrels, organs, cymbals, psaltery, harp and other

29. *Music and Dancing*

stringed instruments). It is interesting to note in the picture, as well as in Scripture, that those of the same sex danced together.

SPORTS

Sports entered into the lives of the ancients. Boxing and wrestling also had a religious significance. Ceremonial wrestlers are shown (*No. 30*) struggling with jars on their heads. Battles were often depicted in such a manner between a hero and a demon. Next time you go bowling, give thought to this striking fact: the Egyptians, several millenniums B.C., started the ball rolling! *No. 31* shows a gaming board (2500 B.C.), which is, no doubt, an ancestor of our modern "dice," so frequently used in games (and otherwise).

Athletics as such had little part in ancient man's way of life. However, physical strength and ability were highly regarded in war. It was left to the olympic games of Greece and the contests of Rome to give to sports its importance. The Greeks enjoyed racing, boxing and

30. *The Wrestlers*

31. *Gaming Board*

wrestling, and throwing the javelin and discus. Rome "honored" sports by giving as many as 135 days a year to it. Chariot racing was popular. Gladiators fought against each other or wild beasts. The Romans favored excitement, danger and bloodshed.

MORALS

Early man's morals were just about the same then as they are today. We have already mentioned laws and the punishment for offenses. A clay tablet hints at "juvenile delinquency" — telling of a father who berated his son for inhuman behavior and ingratitude. Found also in Palestine recently was a pottery bathtub, containing a skull and bones all jumbled together. Probably the newsboy of that day shouted: "Read All about Bathtub Murder! Man Kills Wife While Taking Bath!"

While murder is as old as Cain (Gen. 4:8), the use of intoxicating beverages is also an ancient evil. It is first mentioned in the Bible when Noah got drunk (Gen. 9:20, 21). This would indicate a weakness before the flood, when the heart of man was evil continually (Gen. 6:5). Clay models (*No. 32*) show early use of grain in beer making. The man (right) is shucking the grain while the woman is preparing the mash for brewing. No doubt Noah had a winepress in his vineyard. Ripe grapes were crushed by men treading them. As the juice flowed into an opening, it was scooped up and bottled in jars or wineskins. *No. 33* shows a winepress about five feet long, two feet wide and ten inches deep. The arrow points to an opening where the juice was caught. In larger vats, the treaders would hold to overhead ropes so they would not slip.

The great Greek historian, Herodotus, has been called the "Father of History" by many Bible critics. Statements by him are readily accepted because they contradict many historical records mentioned in Scripture. One such remark was that the Egyptians grew no grapes and drank no wine. Genesis 39 and 40 mention the chief cupbearer of Pharaoh. This cupbearer tells of a dream in which he is standing by a vine and squeezing grapes in a cup. Bible critics might still be siding with Herodotus if a painting had not been found in an Egyptian tomb. It shows natives engaged in winemaking! Some are cultivating and tending the crops, some are dressing and pruning vines, while others are gathering grapes and taking them to the winepress. Men are treading grapes in the vat and others are storing the juice in jugs and wineskins. Another scene depicts a gathering at a banquet table. The artist drew a true-to-life picture, giving evidence that the wine was fermented. Many guests look like the wine is or has been taking effect, and one "society dame" has made her way to a corner to dispose of the effects of her weak stomach. A slave is seen holding a silver bowl to catch the surplus matter. As the banquet comes to a close many banqueteers are being helped home by their slaves. One poor soul has fallen under the table and is overlooked. It looks like Herodotus was absolutely wrong about wine in Egypt.

The word "wine" in the Scriptures is a "generic" term, and is often used for fresh grape juice, as well as for fermented wine. It refers more often to strong drink (Prov. 20:1). A Nazarite was not to drink the "liquor of grapes" (Num. 6: 2, 3), and Habakkuk pronounced a "woe" on any who might cause others to "hit the bottle" (Hab. 2:15). Wine was commonly used to quench thirst because drinking water was scarce, or often contaminated.

RELIGIONS

The Apostle Paul best describes early man's religions and the results which follow when God is dethroned (Rom. 1:21-32). This description by Paul would be hard to believe unless archaeology had revealed evidence to support his claims — and, if we were not living in days such as Noah's before the flood (Matt. 24:37-39), and in times such as Lot's after the flood (Luke 17:28-30). Ever since Cain insisted on going to God "his" way, man in general has gone the "way of Cain" (Gen. 4:4, 5; Jude 11). There

32. *Beer Making*

33. *Winepress*

34. Sun-god Altar

35. Graven Image

is some evidence that the sun was man's first object of worship when he turned away from God. *No. 34* is an image of a sun-god, seated with outstretched arms, ready to receive a sacrifice as the worshiper gazes heavenward to pay homage to the sun, moon, and stars.

Clay tablets tell of religions and gods by the score. Idols — images of gods — varying in size and shape, have been discovered, and reveal that man was polytheistic in belief. He had gods (plural) for all areas of his life — including seasons, rain, harvest, storm, war, sex and wine. *No. 35* is an ancient image, overlaid with finely beaten gold. It stands about four inches high. When early man changed the glory of the living God into images such as Paul mentioned, we see proof of man's love for sin. Gods were made evil so that man might practice sin under their approval and patronage. Practically all man's deities were the product of depraved passions and guilty fears — such as intemperance, lust, jealousy, hate and revenge. Man also began to worship four-footed beasts and creeping things. The whole land of Egypt was covered with temples and buildings dedicated to dogs, lions, birds, crocodiles and beetles. We need only to be reminded that in India today the cow and monkey are sacred, and that an Indian will starve before offending one of these "gods."

While evolutionists would pick man up from some mudhole of the past and elevate him to a place of dignity, man has demonstrated that he is the type who will

37. *Nude Priest*

36. *Goddess of Fertility*

stoop to any level so he does not have to acknowledge his Maker. Satan surely did a good job making man "hit bottom," both in the flesh and spirit. *No. 36* is a "fertility" goddess (the original "pin-up" girl), using four-footed beasts in worship. *No. 37* is a nude priest pouring some ointment on an altar of sacrifice. *No. 38* shows a prostitute priestess on a lion, ready to perform her "act of worship." One account mentions a sex-act between a god and a heifer. Both men and women committed unnatural sex-acts. Nothing is more sinful and wicked than the act of sodomy. Its very meaning is "licentious idolatry." What a blight on the human race that a city (Sodom) had a name related to this sin!

Girls used a "serpent" headdress while performing (*No. 39*). A statue was found of a priestess kissing a snake as it coiled around her waist and breast. (In a California night club, "not even a nip on the back by her pet boa could keep 'topless' dancer Tara from performing" — UP, 7/16/66.) A libation vase (*No. 40*) with serpent designs, was used for

38. *"Sacred" Priestess*

39. *Snake Dancers*

41. Man-headed Serpent

42. Demon Idol

40. Libation Vase

pouring oils upon sacrifices (2000 B.C.).
No. 41 is an Egyptian representing himself as a man-headed serpent in re-incarnation. Man's vain imagination created a demon-god (*No. 42*). Worship
turned from God, to man, to beast, to
creeping things, to Satan.

The Bible stands as a testimony that
not all men rejected God. Adam accepted the provision which God made
for him (Gen. 3:21). Godly Seth's line

produced a man like Enoch, who walked with God (Gen. 5:22). Noah found grace in the eyes of the Lord when all mankind had forsaken righteousness (Gen. 6:8). Abraham was called by God to leave idolatrous Ur of the Chaldees and he became the "Friend of God" (James 2:23). Moses was known as the "man of God" (Deut. 33:1). David was known as a man after God's own heart (Acts 13:22), and through his flesh came the Lord Jesus Christ (Rom. 1:1-4). Faithfulness on the part of godly men down through the centuries (Heb. 11) led to the coming of the Saviour for sinful men. Indebted as we are to mankind's culture in general, none compares with the evidence left by those who kept a knowledge of God in their minds and walked according to His statutes. Since we are compassed about with so great a cloud of witnesses, let us live this life of faith in the midst of a crooked and perverse generation, "looking unto Jesus the author and finisher of our faith" (Heb. 12:1, 2; Phil. 2:15).

SICKNESS, MEDICINES, AND DEATH

While it is not safe to say that all sickness is "of the devil" (see Deut. 29:22), it is reasonable to assume that bodily sickness came as a result of sin. Man not only died spiritually in his disobedience to God, but a death-process began in his body (Gen. 2:17; 3:17-19), and from man's first parents has come our being "born unto trouble" (Job 5:7; 14:1; Eccles. 2:22, 23).

Ancient Mesopotamians believed sickness was either a punishment for sin by a god or due to demon possession, not a pathological disorder. While we are germ conscious, they were "demon" conscious, having classified more than six thousand demons as causes for sickness. Because sickness was considered to be related to their gods and the devil, practice of medicine was limited to priests. Temple priestesses often served as "nurses," assisting the "doctors" and tending to the needs of patients. There were "herb" doctors, or general practitioners; "knife" doctors, or surgeons; and "spell" doctors (we call them "psychiatrists" today). Some prescriptions, to be taken orally, were nauseating and revolting, to say the least. Dog's dung, human excreta and urine were given, not so much to "cure" the patient, but in the hope that the demons would be expelled. However, these ancients used many herbs and minerals comparable to ours in theraputic value. Belladonna was used to check bladder spasms and poppy was administered for pain and to produce sleep. We profit today by their graphic accounts of eye diseases, jaundice, fevers, and their ideas on the spread of disease. Records reveal that they even had their own "Physical Fitness Program." They went in for such manly exercises as boxing and wrestling and swimming (the beginner used inflated animal bladders as "water-wings"). They carried umbrellas to protect their eyes from the blazing sun and wore "fly-flaps" to repel pesky insects.

The early Egyptians had a large pharmacopoeia and were more advanced than the Mesopotamians. Two documents have been discovered which tell of medical practices: (1) the "Ebers Papyrus," which deals with internal diseases and (2) the "Edwin-Smith Papyrus," the oldest surgical document known. This treatise analyzes many disorders common to man, such as wounds, dislocations, fractures, tumors, ulcers and abscesses. In surgery, lint was used for absorbents, and adhesive plaster or stitching was used to close incisions. Salves were used extensively on wounds. Artificial teeth were also common to the

Egyptians. The Egyptians had a knowledge of a "magic" fluid in the body of man. They knew that the pulsation of the heart was in every vessel, and that loss of blood could be fatal. The Bible records this fact of the circulatory system of the body — "the life of all flesh is in the blood" (Lev. 17:14).

Inherent in every man is the desire to live. This has been proved by the protective methods he has devised for survival and the medicines he has concocted for healing. Knowing the danger of illness and disease, God promised Israel that none of the diseases of the Egyptians would befall her if she obeyed Him (Exod. 15:26). Hygenic laws and certain foods are recorded in the book of Leviticus for the sake of Israel's health. In II Chronicles 16:12 we read of a king seeking physicians for healing. Hezekiah begged not to die, and a poultice of figs was applied to his boil for healing (II Kings 20:1-7).

But, alas, man dies. Death has stalked the earth ever since Adam was driven from the garden of Eden. "In Adam all die" (I Cor. 15:22a). Genesis 5 has been called the "graveyard" of early man. Death has been no respector of persons, and from graves and tombs has come evidence of this fact. Since man in general has always believed in a future life, many personal belongings and funerary texts buried with the dead give us much information as to the manner of preparation for burial, the burial itself, and much of their religious beliefs concerning death. Egypt devised a method of embalming, or mummification, which we will consider in a later chapter. The "Egyptian Book of the Dead" reveals Osiris (god of the dead and life after death) witnessing a dog-headed scribe weighing the heart of a "candidate" for heaven against a figure symbolizing truth (*No. 43*). Seated on top of the scales is a baboon, the symbol of wisdom. How true of so many today, hoping that their good deeds will outweigh their bad ones, thus meriting God's approval for heaven!

Royal tombs at Ur revealed an elaborate burial system for kings and the

43. Book of the Dead

44. *"John Doe"*
and Earthly
Possessions

wealthy. Not only were they dressed in
full regalia, but their servants, buried
alive with them, were standing ready to
serve. The soldiers were standing at "attention," fully clothed in their armor.
Others "just" died, and were buried in
common graves. The sands of time and
dryness of climate have preserved many
such bodies and personal belongings for
us to observe today (*No. 44*).

The burial of a child was a simple
matter in some cases. The child, having
been dressed in a ceremonial gown, was
slipped through the opening of a large
jar, which served as a coffin (*No. 45*).
Ankle bracelets of metal were left on the
child, and a "burial juglet," filled with
food for life in the future, was placed
nearby. The "columbarium" (*No. 46*)
shows that cremation was not unknown.
Bodies were placed on a pyre, and the
ashes were gathered to be scattered or
placed in jars. This unearthed "vault"
shows a number of niches for cinerary
urns.

Modern man is inclined to overlook
the fact that ancient man *was* civilized.
Evidence presented in this chapter is
proof of early man's ability to live with
the essentials of life. Now that we are
acquainted with this knowledge of man
from the "cradle to the grave," let us pro-
ceed to our next chapter — "Digging Up
What's Down" — to see how most of this
information came to light.

45. *Jar Burial*

46. *Columbarium*

CHAPTER 2

Digging Up What's Down

Believe it or not, but the Science of Archaeology is comparatively new. In the early and middle 1800's, archaeological excavations were nothing more than "treasure hunts." The archaeologists kept only those discoveries of precious metals and unbroken pottery. Pottery fragments, skeletons, wall and house foundations, and even different types of pottery found in different levels of civilization were of no value to them. As a result no records of findings were kept in the early stages of this science. Discoveries in these early excavations were taken out of the countries in which they were found; and that is why, for example, one can find more of ancient Greece in the British Museum than he can find in Grecian Museums.

Today, however, the picture is vastly different. The governments of countries where "digs" are conducted require permits to excavate, and their Departments of Antiquity have prior claim on *all* findings for their own museums. What they do not keep, the sponsors of the expedition may take back to their own museums. Items put on display in these "foreign" museums give credit to the college, university, or society which sponsored and conducted the excavations.

Techniques have been developed which have modernized archaeology. While the "tools" seem primitive — picks and shovels, trowels, pen-knives and paint brushes — there are all the advantages of modern science with which archaeologists might arm themselves. Aerial cameras detect faint outlines of crumbled walls, and air-borne magneto-meters ferret out demolished fortifications. Many findings will yield to the scientific laboratory: fossilized grains of pollen tell of the climate in which they grew; tiny bits of carbon assist in establishing dates; mummies yield to autopsy for information of ancient diseases; and re-used writing material, called "palimpsests," are put to the ultraviolet ray which reveals messages erased thousands of years ago. Modern archaeology is an intricate and cooperative effort to give a new library about man's past.

Present-day expeditions are made up of a director and several staff members, including area crew supervisors, draftsman, photographer, and a pottery expert (*No. 47*). The director maps out areas where the crew will dig, and works with the surveyor in "staking the claim" (*No. 48*). From then on he supervises everything. Day after day he goes from level to level comparing the results in one area with another, correlating the findings so that ultimately he may connect them in a single coherent unit. He must see that no bottleneck develops anywhere. When pickmen or basket-carriers are slow, or pottery sorters and recorders retard, there will be no baskets for those on the mound, and no work for others. Like an "assembly line," no one dares lag behind. Every night the director must go over plans and diagrams to decide what should be done the next day, what walls to preserve or remove.

The first season's dig at a given site has a limited objective — to determine the stratification of the mound; that is, the different periods of occupation from

47. Staff Members

the first settlement until the last city was abandoned. The side of the slope is selected for this project. Three areas are usually marked off, one on top and two on the side. Crews dig shafts in each area, leaving solid partitions of untouched material in between. As the shafts go downward, each wall exposes thousands of years of occupancy, until the men strike "virgin soil," where no further evidence of civilization is found. (Of course, all "artifacts" or objects found in these test-shafts are kept and recorded.) By "sounding" the slope of the tell the chief archaeologist is then able to determine the number of cities buried on this one site. The next season he will move to the top of the mound, remove the surface soil (*No. 49*), then peel off the layers of human occupation and reconstruct each city in the process. *No. 50* is a diagram of a layer in marked-off areas.

Unskilled labor is employed for the digging, and the Labor Office supplies a list of men from the neighboring towns. Each area consists of a crew of ten to twelve (*No. 51*). At Dothan we worked three areas, employing about thirty-five

48. Staking an Area

49. *Removing Surface Soil*

Jar Burial
 	
A-112
	x Adult
	   Skeleton
	Large
	Zirs x x
	A-109
		N
		↑
		86'
		x
		78'
			Inscribed x
			Handles
			   x
			Hellenistic
			Lamp
			  ◓ A-106
				Stone
				Door
				Socket
				Silver
				Coins
				  ✿ A-103

Flints x x
   x
 	
A-111
	Plastered
	Storage Bins
	◯◯
	
	A-108
		To
		D
		u
		m
		p
			BRICK
			KILN
			
			A-105
				❀ Sling
				  Stones
				Olive
				Press
				⬡ A-102

Spindle Whorls ◖◗ A-110	Potter's House A-107	A r e a ↓	Pinch-lip Lamp ◗ Charred Grain ✿ A-104	20' X 26' Saddle Quern ⬭◯ A-101

50. *Marked-off Areas*

51. *Area Crew*

52. *"Scooping" Dirt*

53. *Carrying Dirt*

men. Two of each crew are trained, one using a pick to dig cautiously when an artifact comes into view, and the other digging under the watchful eye of the supervisor so as not to damage anything with his "shovel" pick. One "scoops" the dirt into baskets (*No. 52*), and the rest carry the dirt to the dump area (*No. 53*). Just before the dirt is "scooped" into the *gufa* (a basket made from an old rubber tire), the supervisor has made sure that no small object (coin, bead, etc.) has escaped. Sometimes a sieve is used for sifting dirt, making sure that nothing is overlooked.

The dump area (*No. 54*) is usually located at the edge of the slope, where, the director hopes, there is nothing of importance beneath. He lives in fear that he may be covering a gate entrance into the city, or a building of importance. This happened in ancient Assyria (Iraq) when it was learned that the dump area covered a palace (which was later unearthed).

An important factor in any excavation is a good relationship between the staff and crew. Language is a barrier, but signs often assist. One member in our crew started work each day with a song. (At least he called it that!) One morning I sang along with him and thereafter

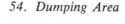

54. *Dumping Area*

55. *"Songs at Sunrise"*

them to see if any have painted marks (*No. 56*). Designs, marks, etc., are often characteristic of certain ages. Odd things come to light — such as a "stone door socket" (*No. 57*). In the construction of a house or building, a socket was fitted into the foundation. As the wall was built upward, a pole was placed in the lower socket and another socket capped the pole (*No. 58*). A door was placed in the opening; metal or wood strips were nailed to both door and pole, and the pole became the hinge. Large stone door sockets used for stone doors have been discovered. A notch on the "hinge" side of the door was at the top and bottom. Stone doors were common in Lot's day (No. 114).

we started each day with "Songs at Sunrise" (*No. 55*). Anyone not able to carry a tune can sing in Arabic. No. 52 also shows a good relation between members of the staff and crew.

When digging actually gets underway, surface or top soil is removed (No. 49). Very soon potsherds appear. When large pieces are viewed, water is poured on

A digger called to our attention that he had struck a large deposit of clay. Nearby was a brick kiln, and huge bricks, 21 x 15 x 5½ inches. A broken brick gave evidence of a stray goat who had wandered in the brick yard while they were drying (*No. 59*). Little did he dream history would expose his footprint centuries later! Another area yielded wall foundations of houses and buildings as seen in *No. 60*. These same large bricks had been used in the construction of houses in this section of the city.

56. *Painted Potsherds*

57. *Stone Door Socket*

58. *Door in Sockets*

59. *"Goat-track" Brick*

No. 61 is a fancy oil cruse. This item was a "must" in every home. Olive oil, stored in cruses, was mixed with flour in cooking and baking. (Remember Elijah and the barrel of meal? — I Kings 17: 12). Oil cruses were used by the five "wise" virgins who had an extra supply of oil (Matt. 25:4). Notice their type of oil cruse in No. 272. Cruses varied in sizes and shapes, from a few ounces to a quart.

60. *House and Wall Foundations*

61. *Fancy Oil Cruse*

62. *Ostracon*

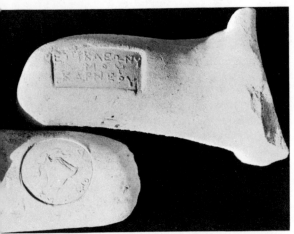

63. *Inscribed Jar Handles*

64. *Multiple-handle Bowl*

The delight of all archaeologists is the discovery of an inscribed object — a stele (inscribed monument), a clay tablet, or an ostracon (*No. 62*). Ostraca are pottery fragments used as inexpensive writing material. The potsherd was inscribed with ink, and used for brief messages, letters, receipts, school texts, etc. *No. 63* shows two inscribed Rhodian wine jar handles, one saying — *"To the praise of my new wine."* These handles are dated in the Hellenistic period, about 300 B.C.

In excavations at the Old Testament site of Lachish, eighteen "Lachish letters" were found (similar to the one in No. 62). These letters contained information of political and military situations prior to the destruction of Jerusalem by Nebuchadnezzar. One letter refers to a messenger making a trip to Egypt for help and to a letter written by a royal officer, with a warning from a prophet (possibly Jeremiah). Also found was a seal: *"To Gedaliah who is over the house"* (probably one of Judah's last prime ministers). See No. 220.

No. 64 shows a "multiple handle" bowl *in situ* (in the actual location in which it was found). Such a bowl would correspond to our punch bowl today. The handles were spaced about three inches apart, and every fourth handle was in the shape of an animal. *No. 65* shows the "multiple handle" bowl after it was restored. The pieces were put together by a "jig-saw" pottery expert.

The finding of coins is not at all uncommon (*No. 66*). The use of coins began about 500 B.C. Pictured (lower left) is a silver Roman eagle. Others are first-century bronze coins. The two small coins beneath the American half-dollar are the "widow's mites" (Mark 12:41-44). Above is a Jewish coin which was minted in the Hellenistic period, about 300 B.C.

65. Bowl Restored

When the archaeologist reaches the bottom of the first "occupational level" (*No. 67*), he can reconstruct this part of the city. In view is a plastered floor, plastered storage bins, wall foundations, etc. An excellent find is a "plastered floor" (*No. 68*), which is the opposite of

66. Jewish and Roman Coins

67. Occupational Level

68. Plastered Floor

69. *Plastered Storage Bins*

70. *The Photographer*

our plastered ceiling. *No. 69* is a close-up of plastered storage bins. The plaster has been preserved due to dry climate and its being completely sealed off from the air. Grain was usually stored in this size bin. A photographer (*No. 70*) is on hand to photograph all objects *in situ,* and especially to take as many angle shots of an occupational level as are needed for the director later to review the area and correlate the findings of levels in one area with levels in another. Ofttimes a ladder "brigade" comes to the photographer's aid for his shots. A drawing board (*No. 71*) is also essential. The draftsman's pen is ready to make accurate drawings of each occupational level — every object's location, etc. Nothing can be left to guess work, for government officials will come to inspect the digging, to check records and to look over the findings. Archaeology is an "irreversible" science, i.e., it destroys one

71. *Drawing Board*

72. Breaking Stones

level as it proceeds to the next (*No. 72*). It is obvious why drawings must be made and photographs taken.

A major find at any excavation is a city wall (*No. 73*). Here a few stones were jutting just above the surface soil. Noticing that the pile of rocks became larger as we removed the dirt, it became evident that we were unearthing the city wall. *No. 74* shows the top and outside section of the wall of Dothan. This is the same wall seen by Elisha and his servant (II Kings 6). A six-foot square hole was opened at the inside of the wall to determine its height (*No. 75*), and at the same time some men were clearing the dirt from the top and outside of the wall to learn its width. After digging into "virgin soil" (in which we found no fur-

73. Finding City Wall

75. Bottom of City Wall

74. Top of City Wall

76. *City Set on a Hill*

ther evidence of occupation), we measured the wall from top to bottom — twenty-two feet high, and eleven feet wide.

WHERE SHALL WE DIG?

A mound of ancient occupation is often identified by its shape and the amount of pottery that is found on its top. The shape is distinctive — like an "upside-down" cone, flattened on top and steep on the sides. This shape came into being when a city, encircled by a wall, was built on a natural hill (*No. 76*). With the abandonment or downfall of this original city, walls erode and buildings cave in, but sufficient rubble is left to form the foundation for the building of the next city. Over a period of time the mound gradually becomes higher but its area becomes much smaller, until it is no longer suitable for habitation. Some mounds have reached a height of seventy feet, and contain as many as twenty-two different cities, each representing a different period of history. Outside the wall most of the debris has rolled down the hill, but inside is the debris of successive cities, waiting for some archaeologist to dig up what's down.

Most Biblical sites have remained the same since the first city was built. In the case of Dothan (*No. 77*), located about sixty miles north of Jerusalem and mentioned twice in the Bible (Gen. 37:17, when Joseph was sold by his brothers to Egyptian merchantmen, and II Kings 6:

77. *"Tell" Dothan*

78. Solomon's
Copper Mines

13-17, when Elisha and his servant saw the Lord's army on the mountainside), its location has been established for centuries, not only by tradition, but by its location in relation to other Biblical cities such as Megiddo and Samaria. One look at Dothan's mound will convince the observer that it is not a "natural" mountain. The flatness of the top and the terraced slope is sufficient proof of buried layers of stratification. However, some tells have eroded to such a degree that the huge collection of potsherds is the only evidence that a city once existed on that site.

With Bible in hand, it is comparatively easy for the archaeologist to locate sites in the Holy Land. For example, I Kings 7:45, 46 mentions copper vessels made for Solomon's temple. If the mines from which Solomon got this copper every existed, they had disappeared from the memory of man for almost three thousand years. After searching for twenty years, archaeologist Nelson Glueck found a ruined site the natives traditionally called "Copper Ruin." He excavated. Crumbled walls and furnaces black with heaps of copper slag proved to be a once great copper smelter. Further south were found seven similar centers. Pottery in all of them was from the time of Solomon. At last the famous copper mines of king Solomon had been discovered! Glueck also followed the Biblical description of an ancient city — "Ezion-geber . . . beside Eloth on the shore of the Red Sea in the land of Edom" (I Kings 9:26) — and located "the Pittsburgh of Palestine." Here, in the center of a geographical rift, furnaces took advantage of the strong wind blowing down this natural corridor to fan flames as they refined the ore. Solomon's "copper mines" still produce ore, and are operated today by his kinsmen (No. 78). Israel *is* a "land out of whose hills thou mayest dig brass [copper]" (Deut. 8: 7-9).

The Bible tells us that the cities of Sodom and Gomorrah were destroyed by fire and brimstone (Gen. 19:24, 28). Excavations at the southern end of the Dead Sea (No. 79) show the whole area to have been destroyed by a volcanic eruption some two thousand years B.C. The whole place proved to be a burned-out region of oil and asphalt. Formerly, there had been a subterranean lake of oil and gas beneath these cities. Taking the verses of Sodom's destruction literally, business men said the rising flames of verse 28 meant natural gas. Natural gas indicates oil, and the drilling of Israel's first oil well started in 1953.

In the forbidding Negev desert region

DEAD

SEA

●-Sodom

●-Gomorrah

79. *The Dead Sea*

south of Beer-sheba, no settlement had existed since about A.D. 600. Genesis 21:22-34 implies that Abraham had great herds in this region. From where had water for grazing land and for animals come? Archaeologists took a close look at the hills and even the smallest gullies. There they found the remains of dikes, all woven into an intricate drainage system which conserved every drop of rain water. Reading that Isaac had dug wells in that same area (Gen. 26: 17-19; *No. 80*), many were found and these "stopped-up" wells were cleaned out. The Jews of today are making the "desert blossom as the rose" because the Bible is helping to discover wells and irrigation ditches.

When fighting broke out between the Jews and the Arabs in 1947, the Bible brought to light a similar invasion by Israel against Syria twenty-eight hundred years ago (II Sam. 8:5, 6; 10:17-19). Believing that the terrain would force a similar invasion route, the Israelites familiarized themselves with the countryside and the Biblical details of that battle

80. *Ancient Well*

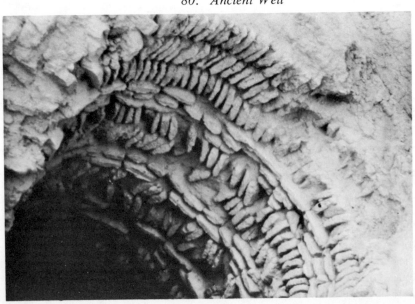

centuries ago. As expected, the Syrians followed the same route and the Jewish soldiers won the battle over Syria. The Bible also helped to discover an ancient road going toward Egypt's central garrison. Under cover of darkness the Israelies sped along this ancient route and took the Egyptians by surprise. Their defense system was knocked out of commission and as a result the war ended sooner than expected.

The "Six Days' War" (June, 1967), in which Israel overwhelmingly defeated three Countries — Syria, Jordan, and Egypt — was due largely to these same tactics, plus their lightning-speed attack. Israel's sea-port city of Eilat was idled because Egyptian forces on the Sinai peninsula had closed the Gulf of Aqaba to all shipping. Jordanian soldiers were threatening Jerusalem and the Syrians were pressing from the north near the Sea of Galilee. The Arabs had vowed to drive Israel into the Mediterranean Sea, but the Israeli air-force knocked out Egypt's air-force on the ground and their tanks followed old Biblical paths through the Negev desert to rout the Egyptians from Sinai. Similarily, Israeli forces stormed the old Biblical valleys and hills surrounding Jerusalem to capture Jordan's part of the Old City, and soon the Syrian army surrendered after their land was invaded. This is the first time Jerusalem has been in the hands of an independent Israel since their capture by Nebuchadnezzar of Babylon in 587 B.C.

HOW CITIES AND OBJECTS BECOME BURIED

It might come as a surprise to some that drifting sand is but a small factor in the burial of an ancient city. In desert regions this might contribute a part, but the main reason is the repeated destruction and the rebuilding of the city on the *same* site. Cities were built near springs and waterholes; and instead of moving to another location, the custom was to rebuild the city on the old site, salvaging what stones and materials were usable. The chief reason for continuing on the old site was not the ease with which this could be done, or because the water supply was there already, but the desire to follow, wherever possible, the outline of old buildings, particularly temples, to earn the protection of the gods and spirits that the previous inhabitants had pacified.

Many factors determined a city's destruction. Disease often wiped out many of the inhabitants, and the survivors would abandon the site. When a village became abandoned, stone and mud houses would collapse, fences would fall down, stray animals would uproot soil, terraces would disintegrate, sand and debris would clog wells and springs, and winds would pile up debris and refuse in the streets. Later, when others reoccupied the city site, another level would be added in their erection of a new city. Fire would often destroy a city. Picture No. 60 points out an ash layer, giving evidence of a fire. Many times these nomadic people would rather move to a new location than remain to clear the burnt debris and begin anew at their old homesite. Then such a city would lie waste, possibly for many years before others would resettle. Earthquakes often contributed to a city's destruction (*No. 81*).

Possibly the method most employed in

81. Earthquake

82. Battered Skeleton

the destruction of a city was war, which is always devastating (No. 20). Complete victory came about when battering rams crumbled walls and fires leveled buildings. Jericho's destruction is a good example of this. The conquerors set it afire, and another city was brought to naught (Josh. 6:24). When excavations are in progress, often a battered skeleton (*No. 82*) will be found at the base of a demolished wall, giving mute evidence of violence, possibly brutality in waging war. Shellac is applied immediately to newly exposed bones to preserve them, since exposure to air and light causes them to disintegrate in a short time. This individual's skull was crushed, collarbone broken, knees bent backward toward the stomach and broken, and a fist clenched. When a doctor visited our dig at Dothan, we asked him for information as to age, sex, and probable cause of death. We watched as he probed around, stroked his chin, grunted a time or two, and then concluded that at some time during this man's life he had died!

From a Biblical viewpoint, these contributing factors of destruction, especially war, were but methods chosen sometimes by God, either because (1) heathens refused to repent; (2) enemies mocked God and His dwelling place or sought to destroy His people; or (3) because of sins in the lives of those who named His name.

The annihilation of Sodom and Gomorrah and Babylon's downfall are examples of God's judgment because of moral and spiritual conditions (Gen. 19; Isa. 13: 19-22). Jonah was used of God to spare a city (Nineveh) when its people repented and believed God (Jonah 1:2; 3:1-10). The city of Tyre is a long forgotten city because its king spoke out against Jerusalem. At one time it was one of the world's mightiest cities, so strong that the king of Assyria, Sennacherib, failed to conquer it after beseiging it for thirteen years. It was stormed by another mighty power, Nebuchadnezzar of Babylon, and he failed. Yet God prophesied that Tyre's walls would be broken, her pleasant houses destroyed, and the stones of the city be in the midst of the water (Ezek. 26: 1-14). Alexander the Great fulfilled God's Word in destroying the city. Today, all the archaeologist can find of Tyre are stones along the shore, used for drying fish nets, and washed by the waves as tides ebb and flow. Archaeology's discovery at this site confirms the fulfillment of Ezekiel's prophecy.

Many warnings were given to Israel regarding her disobedience to God and the consequences of her sins — one of which was that her cities would become waste, or destroyed (Lev. 26:31, 33). Many cities of Judah fell before Shishak, king of Egypt, because Israel "transgressed against the Lord" (II Chron. 12: 2, 5). Israel despised God's Word, misused His priests, and did His prophets harm. Because of this, God "brought upon them" Nebuchadnezzar, king of Babylon, who battered down the walls of Jerusalem and leveled the city with fire (II Chron. 36:15-21).

Incidentally, an example of the destruction of a city and its being rebuilt on the same site is Jerusalem. One complete destruction came at the hands of

Nebuchadnezzar and another by Titus in A.D. 70. Over seventy years after the Babylonians destroyed the city, Nehemiah rallied Israel to build a new wall and city gates on the old locations (Neh. 1:1—6:15). Ezra came back from captivity to build again the temple of God on the old site (Ezra 1:1—6:18). The layer of occupation on which Nehemiah and Ezra built was more than seventy years old, and some of the artifacts of that level differ from many the Israelites brought back from her Babylonian captivity.

TELLING TIME WITH POTSHERDS

In a sense, the evaluation of an archaeological expedition depends upon an accurate recording of the pottery discovered. How then can an archaeologist determine the age of pottery — or — how does pottery determine the age of a given level?

Sir Flinders Petrie, a noted Egyptologist, established the pattern of pottery chronology which archaeologists now generally follow. While examining a site called Tell el Hesi, southwest of Jerusalem, he noted the side of the mound was eroded by rain and weather, and many levels were exposed. The potsherds in the lowest level differed from those in the second level. Those in the third level were different from those in the second, and so on. Petrie's discovery revealed a pottery change from level to level. Datable Egyptian artifacts found at Tell el Hesi made it possible to give a rough date to the level in which they were found. The level beneath this "dated" level was, of course, older, and the one above it was a later date. It became evident in these levels that different styles of pottery had been the fashion, making it possible to identify forms unique to each level. Coins and rare bits of writing also helped to place potsherds in a timetable.

On the basis of his discoveries at this site, Petrie showed the relation of objects to each other within their respective levels, and paved the way for the archaeologist of today to date these objects by pottery form and texture, design, decorations and manufacturing techniques. Dating is generally made to within fifty to one hundred years. While the radioactive carbon 14 test assists in dating, potsherds can tell time more accurately.

Styles of decorations or design would come and go and each was usually characteristic of a given age. From the times before Abraham (3000-2100 B.C.), one finds "ledge-handled" bowls and water pots. These handles had "finger" impressions to assure a better grip while carrying heavy vessels. (We thought modern man was clever when he invented this type impression for an automobile steering wheel.) An inverted rim was designed to keep water from splashing out, and is called an "anti-splash" jar. A water jug called the "cord-eye" was common at this time. This type container had two solid handles at the spout with small holes drilled in each to insert a cord, so that the canteen could be swung over the shoulder. Some bowls had a top that curved toward the opening to make pouring much easier. This style was called the "hole mouth." Some vessels were shaped by putting the soft clay in a woven basket so that its outside design was a replica of the basket. Lamps in this period varied slightly in size (from 5 to 6 inches in diameter), but design changed from the round rim to the pinched-lip type (No. 24; lamps 1 and 2).

Potters in Abraham's day would use a pointed instrument to make a fishbone design, or would take a comb and "rake" it over the soft surface to give a ribbed

83. *Types of Potsherds*

84. *Finding Potsherds*

"corduroy" design. They would add color to their finest wares by dipping them in a "slip" (clay diluted to a creamy consistency), or by painting a design on a vessel before firing it. Jars that had "double" handles (two handles molded together) and flat bases were common in this period.

A "wishbone-handle" was characteristic of milk bowls having "ladder" designs on the sides (1300 B.C.). If we discover bowls and jugs on which appear red and black concentric circles, we can be sure the Canaanites of Joshua's day ate and drank from them. A "gloss" was applied to pottery in the days of Israel's kings by burnishing them just before firing. The potter used a shell or pebble to mark the surface. Flaring and molded rims, hollow bases and tubular spouts belong to a later date. There are times when "foreign" pottery is found in a tell, and this could indicate ethnic migration.

If our cities were destroyed today and rebuilt on the same site, we would find items characteristic of certain periods. Today, we use a metal frying pan coated with "teflon." But if our mother's home had been buried, we would "dig" up from her level an aluminum frying pan, and underneath would be grandma's level with her iron skillet. So it was also centuries ago with what man had in his own age.

In picture *No. 83*, we see types of pottery from several periods or ages. The "frog-eyes" (upper left) formed a "ledge-handle" with finger impressions (3000 B.C.). Upper center are painted designs of Abraham's day (2000 B.C.). Crisscross burnishing is in the center (1000-800 B.C.). The "herring-bone" design is at the bottom (3000 B.C.), and at the bottom right is a potter's mark, similar to our letter "H" (possibly his initial, maybe named "Herchimer").

During the entire dig, every potsherd is put into a straw basket, which has been "tagged" as to level and area of the discovery (*No. 84*). When the basket is filled, it is carried by a basket boy from the excavation site to a spot designated as the pottery floor. Each basketful is washed separately by the "pottery washer" (*No. 85*). He scrubs sufficiently to remove all dirt but not a painted design or a "slip." He makes sure he keeps the right potsherds for each "tagged" basket so that each piece can be traced back to its "find spot," or to where it was first located (should the director need to check on a given potsherd later).

After careful washing, the sherds are left in a marked area on the pottery floor to dry in the hot sun (*No. 86*), and then one of the area supervisors sorts through them. Of the dozens of fragments in each group only one or two may be of interest. The rest are discarded. Handles, rims and bases, decorated pieces, those different in color or ware, marks, etc. — these catch the eye of the expert. The few selected ones from each basket are boxed and tagged with the code number of the find spot.

A "pottery recorder" (*No. 87*) inks each piece with its location number and then records each numbered piece with a description of its material, firing (whether too long, too short, or just right), design type, marks, etc. The director later examines the day's results. If he sees an abundance of brownish-red ware with a creamy interior, he will date the area from which they were found about 900-700 B.C. This type of pottery was common in Samaria after Israel's kingdom was divided. If he sees inverted rims, or ledge handles, he will know that the level where they were dug is the 3000-2100 B.C. period.

85. *Washing Potsherds*

86. *Drying and Sorting Potsherds*

87. *Recording Pottery*

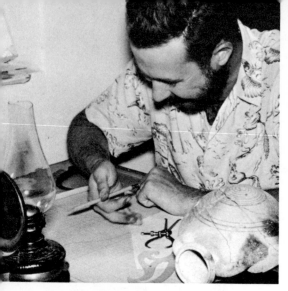

88. *Drawing Objects*

89. *"Put-together" Bowls and Vessels*

Now and then enough fragments of one vessel are found, to make it possible for the "jig saw" expert to restore an object. One of the technicians will take such a restored object, and those found intact, and make a true scale drawing of each (*No. 88*). The photographer also takes pictures of all "put-together" and whole objects. The pictures and drawings are added to other records for further examination. *No. 89* shows "put-together" vessels: left, style and design of Abraham's day; right, concentric circles on jug of Joshua's day; center, Samaritan bowl of king Ahab's time.

While pottery technicians are busy sorting and recording pottery, other staff members are numbering pieces of fallen buildings, including columns and cornices (*No. 90*), which later, when reconstructed, will reveal what the building looked like, its size, etc. The pottery will tell its age and to which period it belonged. To the ancients, pottery was essential to life. It is man's most enduring material. Stone crumbles, metal corrodes, wood decays, and glass disappears. Only pottery will survive. This is why pottery *is* found, and why its forms are so important to the archaeologist.

90. *Pieces of Fallen Building*

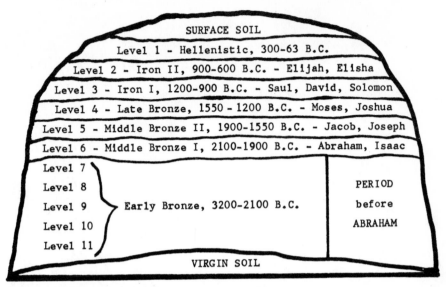

```
                    SURFACE SOIL
          Level 1 - Hellenistic, 300-63 B.C.
      Level 2 - Iron II, 900-600 B.C. - Elijah, Elisha
    Level 3 - Iron I, 1200-900 B.C. - Saul, David, Solomon
      Level 4 - Late Bronze, 1550 - 1200 B.C. - Moses, Joshua
   Level 5 - Middle Bronze II, 1900-1550 B.C. - Jacob, Joseph
   Level 6 - Middle Bronze I, 2100-1900 B.C. - Abraham, Isaac
    Level 7  ⎫
    Level 8  ⎪                                    PERIOD
    Level 9  ⎬  Early Bronze, 3200-2100 B.C.      before
    Level 10 ⎪                                    ABRAHAM
    Level 11 ⎭
                    VIRGIN SOIL
```

91. Diagram of Levels

The levels or periods of civilization (*No. 91*) show the eleven cities of Dothan. The diagram is typical of any dig, no matter how many levels may be discovered or unearthed. *No. 92* best describes a "level." The large, flat stones at the left of arm were a part of a narrow street we unearthed at the bottom of the Hellenistic level (300 B.C.). We left the stones to see how much deeper we would have to dig before coming to the next level. About a foot lower we found a stone door socket, evidence of Iron Age II (900-600 B.C.).

The "STEP TRENCH" (*No. 93*) at Tell Jedeidah, Syria, reveals a series of civilizations superimposed on one another — fourteen distinct "levels of occupation" — 5500 B.C. to A.D. 600.

92. Two Distinct Levels

93. *"Step-trench" Tell*

1. Level of an early Christian Church, Byzantine ruins, A.D. 600-300. Bronze cross.

2. A.D. 300-64 B.C. village. Coins of Roman Caesars and Roman lamps.

3. Level of Greek and Persian Empires, 64-500 B.C. Greek coin.

4. Layers of Syrian Hittite kingdom, 500-1000 B.C. Hittite hieroglyphics.

5. Ceramics of the "Peoples of the Sea," or the Philistines and the Achaeans, 1000-1200 B.C.

6. Imported pottery of Cypriote and Aegean type, 1200-1600 B.C.

7. "Mother-goddess" figurine characteristic of this period, 1600-1900 B.C.

8. Transition period of different types of manufactured pottery, 1900-2000 B.C.

9. Metal and pottery objects, 2000-2300 B.C.

10. Beginning of types of goblets and small drinking vessels; a period of trade between the South and East, 2300-2600 B.C.

11. Period of excellent metalwork; cylinder seals, Mesopotamian type, and fine red and black pottery, 2600-3000 B.C.

12. Casting of human figures in metal, 3000-3500 B.C.

13. Drab pottery and crude metal tools, 3500-3900 B.C.

GAP

---

14. Simple tools in bone and flint, polished pottery, 5000-5500 B.C.

VIRGIN SOIL

Three further questions need to be answered before we consider the discoveries which relate to the Bible.

The first question is "When is the best time to excavate?" Usually, after the rainy season and just before the summer heat sets in. The "season's" dig lasts about three months. If a village is nearby the members of the staff stay in houses; if not, they use tents. Workdays start at sunrise for staff and natives. Due to the afternoon heat the natives quit at 3:30 p.m., but the staff works on pottery, and other discoveries until around 8:00 p.m.

The second question deals with:

HOW INSCRIPTIONS ARE DECIPHERED

Two important discoveries have given us the "keys" to unlock the hieroglyphical style of writing used by the ancient Egyptians, and the cuneiform method used by the ancient Mesopotamians. The Rosetta Stone (*No. 94*), found near Rosetta, Egypt, by an officer of Napoleon's army in 1798, is the one which unlocked the hieroglyphical form. Scholars could read the Greek text at the bottom of the stone. Soon, the Greek personal names were identified in the center text (which is Egyptian demotic, or a written form of the hieroglyphics). Using this as the key to decipher the demotic, scholars soon identified places and the names of kings in the signs and oval frames found in the hieroglyphical text. It was learned that each text — Greek, demotic, hieroglyphic — contained the same message, a decree by priests of Memphis honoring Ptolemy V (203-181 B.C.). The significance is not so much in the decree as in its value in opening the secret of hieroglyphical writings to scholars. *No. 95* shows scholars today copying "yesteryears" headlines from ancient Egyptian buildings.

94. *The Rosetta Stone*

95. *Copying Ancient "Headlines"*

When clay tablets were first brought from Mesopotamia to Europe, scholars wondered if the curious symbols were a form of writing or some form of Near East decoration. It was not until an inscription, recorded by King Darius of Persia in 500 B.C., was discovered (and deciphered), that these symbols were found to be the cuneiform method of writing used by the ancient Mesopotamians. In 1835, Henry Rawlinson, a British officer in the Persian army, was attracted to this rock mountain (*No. 96*; Behistun Rock). About 390 feet above the valley he noticed a smooth section which contained some figures and inscriptions. At great peril to his life he climbed to the point of the carving (*No. 97*). Later he spent four years copying at least twelve hundred lines of the inscription, which was in three languages. Familiar with Persian, and with the aid of clay tablets, he soon noticed such names as Darius, Xerxes, and Hystaspes. By comparison, he made out some of the "signs" which led to the "spelling" of these proper names and translated four hundred lines. It was a record of King Darius I of Persia who ordered the account of his victory over an insurrection in Susa, and how he had led his troops to put down rebellion in Babylon. Darius praised himself frequently. (See p. 159.)

Working on the assumption that the other two languages or inscriptions told the same story, able scholars found their hunch correct. The second text was the old Elamite language, a written form of the cuneiform. This clue was used on the third text, and as names, places and events began to appear, scholars were able to break the back of the "unknown" cuneiform style of writing. To test the results of the findings on the Behistun Rock, the British Museum gave these scholars a copy of an inscription which

96. *Behistun Rock*

97. *Darius' Inscription-Behistun Rock*

had been made by an Assryian king about eleven hundred years before Christ. Each scholar was to work on his unknown document separately. Using the "key" which unlocked the message left by Darius, they brought back their findings at a given time. Surprisingly, each "deciphered" message agreed from start to finish.

We are indebted indeed, first, to the discovery of the Rosetta Stone and Behistun Rock, and second, to scholars who could decipher their messages. Without the information of these two inscriptions from secular history, the critics of the Bible would still be "labeling" false many of the historical claims of the Scriptures.

ARCHAEOLOGICAL PERIODS

Question three deals with archaeological periods. In Palestine, the commonly recognized periods of time are:

THE STONE AGE
Mesolithic
(Natufian) _ca._ 8000-6000 B.C.
Pre-pottery
Neolithic _ca._ 6000-5000 B.C.
Pottery Neolithic_ca._ 5000-4000 B.C.
Chalcolithic _ca._ 4000-3200 B.C.

THE BRONZE AGE
Early Bronze (EB) _ca._ 3200-2100 B.C.
Middle Bronze (MB)
_ca._ 2100-1550 B.C.
Late Bronze (LB) _ca._ 1550-1200 B.C.

THE IRON AGE
Early Iron I _ca._ 1200-900 B.C.
Middle Iron II _ca._ 900-600 B.C.
Late Iron III _ca._ 600-300 B.C.

HELLENISTIC
AGE _ca._ 300- 63 B.C.

ROMAN AGE _ca._ 63 B.C.-A.D. 323

BYZANTINE AGE_ca._ A.D. 323-636

ISLAMIC AGE_ca._ A.D. 636-present

CHAPTER 3

Fables or Facts

When Jesus was making His triumphal entry into Jerusalem, the people began to rejoice and praise God with a loud voice. Some of the Pharisees asked Jesus to rebuke His disciples for this, but He answered, "If the people should hold their peace, the stones would cry out immediately" (Luke 19:37-40). Even though men seek to silence God, He has never been without a witness (Acts 14: 17).

Why "religious" leaders have sought to silence God's witness is one of the mysteries of the ages. Especially since the nineteenth century has this been true when the heirs of the Protestant Reformation began to hold their peace about Christ. They denied His being the Son of God, virgin born. They tore the Bible apart, stating that much of it was myth and folklore. Many passages of Scripture which mentioned specific names, places and events, which were not found in secular history, were considered to be false records. They had a "field day" in their attempt to bring God's Word to the level of man's writings. Soon, a number of our leading Christian Seminaries and Colleges departed from the faith. This resulted in "Modernism" being enthroned, and unquestioning faith in the Bible being looked upon as something that either belongs to the dim ages of the past or in the grave. While the so-called scholarly critic of the Word ridicules believers for their acceptance of the Word by faith, and demanding "proof" at the same time that the Bible is true, God, in a miraculous way, began to employ a Science to come to the rescue of His Word

— the Science of Archaeology. God is literally causing "stones to cry out" in defense of His Word. From a buried past "dead stones with living messages" are beginning to silence the mouths of those who would silence the believer of the Scriptures.

Up until the Science of Archaeology was given to us by God a little over a century ago, virtually all knowledge of the ancient Near East stemmed from the Bible. Nearly all the history of Egyptian, Babylonian, Persian, Assyrian and Hittite empires and kings was accounted for either directly from Biblical narratives, or indirectly from ancient writings which went back to Bible records. Lands, people and customs once known to the Christians from Biblical references only and, strangely, many times, considered mythical or fictional for that reason, are now known to be true because of the unearthing of documents and objects these ancient people made and inscribed. The "pick and spade" of the archaeologist has made the world of the Old and New Testament saints live again. Because of its discovered evidence, archaeology has become a recognized Science by both opponents and proponents of the Scriptures, and its evidence *must* be admitted whether it is accepted or not.

Archaeology's role is of vast importance to the Bible student. In all the discoveries and developments of this Science up to the present moment, not a single thing has been brought to light which contradicts the Word of God. Not all discoveries relate to the Bible, but those which do, especially to historical

65

statements, testify to its trustworthiness. They confirm numerous passages that the critics reject as either fictional, mythological, or not historical and contradictory to "accepted fact." Much of Liberalism's strength was its early "mis-use" of objects unearthed by archaeologists. In all young sciences, "too big conclusions are drawn from too little evidence," and to the Liberal a similarity of records discovered to any account in the Bible meant that the writers of the Bible simply copied them. For example, the Liberal thought because there were similarities of Moses' Law and the Code of Hammurabi, Moses copied his laws from Hammurabi. This supposition was presented as evidence only because Moses lived a few centuries *after* Hammurabi. The Liberals ignored the *differences* of these two sets of laws. The God of Moses' law declared wrong and sinful many evil practices which appeal to man's natural heart, while the "sun-god" of Hammurabi, "Shamash," permitted many practices that are immoral in nature.

Caution should be taken by the Bible believer regarding discoveries which relate directly or indirectly to the Bible. There is a tendency on the part of Christians to use the word "prove" when describing the function of archaeology in relation to the Bible. It has led, for example, to such statements that "flood deposits at Ur of the Chaldees *prove* that the Biblical flood actually occurred." Although clay and silt deposits at Ur (and other cities in that area) indicate a widespread flood, this by itself does not "prove" a flood the nature of which is mentioned in Genesis 7.

Critics of the Bible are also guilty of making such statements. For example: "Recent or present excavations at Jericho 'prove' that no city of importance existed in Joshua's day, although excavations at this site do reveal that a city existed 100 years prior to, and another city existed many years after his day." When another city was rebuilt after its destruction, the newly-built one might contain the same area as the former, it might cover more or less, or it might "overlap" at certain sections. The diagram (*No. 98*) serves to illustrate. The solid line (No. 1) represents a city one hundred years before the Jericho of Joshua's time. The dotted line (No. 2) represents Joshua's city, and the dashes (No. 3) represent a city after Joshua's day. In digging down through No. 3 city at point A, the next city the archaeologist hits is No. 1, completely missing Joshua's city (No. 2). If the archaeologist digs at point B the next season, he will miss No. 2 city again. If he digs at point C the following year, he will "hit" the city of Joshua's day. One can readily see how a city of a given period could be missed. Such a statement as the example above, based on one or two excavations, does not "prove" that a city of Jericho *did not* exist in Joshua's day, because a *series* of excavations have proved that it did.

Sometimes the Bible mentions something which secular history does not. Sometimes an archaeological discovery reveals a historical record which the Bible does not. In either event, one does not discredit or necessarily contradict the other. But when an unearthed record from the past corroborates a statement in the Word of God, we say this "confirms its trustworthiness." If the reader will keep this in mind, he will be careful not to use the expression, "archaeology proves the Bible."

In addition to assisting in confirming many passages of Scripture, the Science of Archaeology provides further light on ancient times and customs. Discoveries make it possible to understand the past, and in turn a knowledge of the past

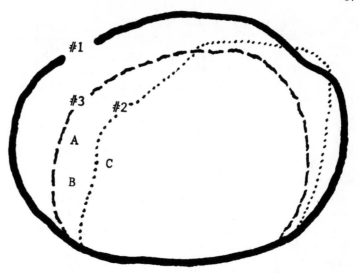

98. City of Jericho

makes meaningful our own civilization. The more one digs, the more he feels that there is "nothing new under the sun." This Science has practically brought to naught the old saying, "Dead men tell no tales." What started out to be a "treasure hunt" has become a Science, and this Science is a literal fulfillment of some stones which "cry out" in praise to the Lord when men's tongues are silent. God refuses to be without a witness, and with such evidence at hand, may we "cry out" to those who refuse to believe the Bible. Or, if we have held our peace in confessing things Biblical, may we not be ashamed to use them to "cry out" in praise to Him who loved us and gave Himself for us.

STONES CRY OUT IN DEFENSE OF CREATION

In records which relate to creation, both Biblical and archaeological, *none mentions or even hints at a theory of evolution.* If the account of creation in the Bible is true (and I believe it is), then God, after writing was invented by man, saw to it that a true record was given. This inspired record by Moses is found in the first and second chapters of Genesis. Although Adam was not present to witness God's creative acts, it is not unreasonable to assume that when God walked with him in the Garden of Eden (Gen. 3:8) that Adam asked countless questions concerning himself and things round about him. Whatever information he received he evidently told his sons and his grandchildren. This is inferred in the sacrifice which Cain and Abel brought to the Lord (Gen. 4:3, 4). How did Abel know what was acceptable to God unless his parents told him? With the retelling of stories over a period of time, addition or deletion is made, and even corruption of said event sets in. Because this is true, we are not surprised at secular records which relate to creation.

Yet, in all of them, there is some similarity to what is found in the Scriptures. When Nineveh was excavated, thousands of clay tablets were discovered which made up the library of King Ashurbanipal of Assyria who reigned *ca.* 650 B.C. When, in 1872, these tablets were deciphered by George Smith of the British Museum, he found a set of seven tablets giving a story of creation, called the "Creation Epic" (one of which is *No. 99*). This account on seven tablets could correspond to the Biblical account of seven days, six of creation and one of rest. On the first tablet there is related a time when the heavens and earth did not exist, when a watery deep or chaos was at the beginning of time and when gods were "born" or began, who represented order and system. There is certainly no similarity here to the God of Genesis 1:1 and these gods, yet there is some similarity of a time when the heavens and earth were not in existence, and when there was a watery deep and chaos.

Another tablet tells of the creation of the stars to mark existing time and the moon to give a specific time for each day. It is implied in this tablet that heavenly bodies precede any creative work of plant or animal life. This corresponds to our fourth day (Gen. 1:14-

99. Creation Epic

19). The sixth tablet is a record of man's creation and the seventh tablet refers to a special day. This corresponds to man's creation on the sixth day (Gen. 1:26-31) and to a special seventh day of rest (Gen. 2:1-3).

Another account of creation has been discovered. It is called the Babylonian Creation account, and relates a gruesome story of gods who assembled themselves in a holy conclave and drunken stupor, and killed one another in jealousy. As in the Creation Epic, there is no similarity of these gods to God, yet there is a striking phenomenon in the outline of this account. Both the Word of God and the Babylonian account have the following order:

1. Primeval chaos.
2. Beginning of light.
3. Creation of the firmament.
4. Appearance of dry land.
5. Creation of luminaries.
6. Creation of man.
7. Deity rests.

While ancient Mesopotamian records of creation reveal some striking similarities of the Bible record, Egyptian accounts show none, except that gods created matter. The nude Sky-goddess Nut (*No. 100*) is arched as the "heavens" over the earth, with the uplifted arms of the air-god Shu supporting her. Shu has the symbol for "year" crowning his head. At his feet lies the earth-god Geb, and ramheaded gods supporting the arms of Shu. Nearby are other gods. The ancient Egyptians also taught that the heavens and earth were generated from some kind of pulp.

Sacred Hindu writings give us this creation account: "Millions of years ago the world came into existence. It was a flat triangular plane with high mountains and many waters. It existed in many

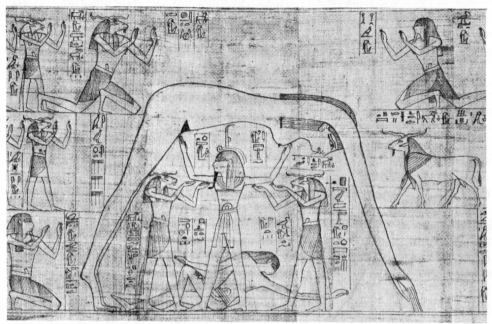

100. Sky-goddess Nut

levels and stories, and was held up upon the heads of elephants who stood on the shell of a tortoise, who in turn stood on the coil of a monstrous serpent. When the elephants shook themselves, the earth would quake and tremble."

If such accounts as these were found in the Bible there would be cause for critics to ridicule God's Word. Such absurd accounts and theories would instantly prove that the Bible was not divinely inspired. If archaeology "proves" anything concerning the accounts in the Bible, it is that they are genuine. If the writings of Moses were a series of myths and fictional tales, their details would be full of errors and contradictions, and we would have to agree with the Modernists and Liberals that they were scientific trash. But thank God His Word is not scientific trash. Early man attributed the origin of the heavens and earth to his gods, and archaeological discoveries tend to support rather than refute the Bible account of "direct creation."

WHEN DID MAN BEGIN?

Man, so the Bible tells us, had a beginning, and at his creation he began as a man who was intelligent, capable of improvement, and who could replenish the earth with offspring "after his kind."

Man, so the evolutionists tell us, evolved from a mess of slimy goo. But all that the evolutionists have done so far is to make an attempt to shake the authority of the Bible and wreck the faith of weak believers. They have not given us the "missing link." Their guesses, inferences, and so-called evidence of evolutionary processes have not amounted to a demonstration. They are not sufficiently agreed to meet in a council and formulate a creed as to the origin of the world and man. Nor are they likely to do so.

The Bible says that God created man

in His own image and likeness (Gen. 1:26, 27). Man is above all creation but still responsible to serve his Creator. He shares in God's nature, but he is not God. To this the evolutionist will not subscribe. To do so he would have to acknowledge God. In his theory man becomes his own god, answerable only to himself.

There is some similarity in archaeological records to the Bible's account of direct creation of man. Egyptian discoveries tell of the god Khnum, who took a "slab" of mud, placed it on his potter's wheel and molded it into the physical form of the first man. Another god, Thoth, stood behind Khnum and marked the span of man's years on a notched twig or branch. The Bible tells us of our God forming man out of the dust of the ground (Gen. 2:7). At least ancient Egyptian records state that man's creation was "direct" — not via the evolutionary route. In the Babylonian Creation account (called the "Enuma-elish"), tablet 6 describes the forming of man from the blood of a god in the presence of other gods. There is a similarity of this to Genesis 1:26 — "Let *us* make man in *our* image." Also, in this account, there is no hint that the first man evolved — rather, he was created.

WHERE DID MAN BEGIN?

Archaeology agrees with the Science of Ethnology (the study of man's origin) that the human race originated in ancient Mesopotamia (modern Iraq). All the real evidence we have — the Bible, archaeology, and the traditions of men — points to this section of the earth as the cradle of civilization, the oldest home of men, and the region where animals, fruit, vegetables, had their origin. The Bible pinpoints "where" man began — in the Garden of Eden, between two rivers, the Hiddekel (Tigris) and the Euphrates (Gen. 2:14). Changing topography renders any precise location now only a guess. Clay tablets found in this area support Eden's location near Eridu, south of Ur. Information from these tablets says that Eridu had a garden in which there was a sacred tree.

In another account giving details of creation (called the "Myth of Adapa"), mention is made of "food for life," which corresponds to a garden where trees for "food" and "life" were planted (Gen. 2:8, 9). This account is similar to the Bible account that eternal life could be obtained by eating this fruit (Gen. 3:22b). In both accounts there is some similarity as to man's suffering and death. At Nineveh there was found a clay impression, showing two figures seated beside a sacred tree, plucking fruit (*No. 101*). A serpent stands behind the woman, erect, as though whispering to her. This seal shows the main features

101. Temptation Seal

of the Biblical story to have been a part of the accepted beliefs of early man.

A clay seal (*No. 102*) was found at Tepe Gawra, near Nineveh, in 1932, and is now located in the University Museum of Pennsylvania. It shows a man and woman walking in a downcast position. E. A. Speiser, who found this seal, said it strongly suggested the story of Adam and Eve being driven from Eden. It is another bit of evidence from archaeology that people other than God's chosen people believed a story closely related to the Garden of Eden account in the Bible.

It is generally conceded by the ethnologist that when races of people hold to a common and strongly developed belief or idea, there must have been a historical event or incident which formed the basis for that traditional belief. With this in mind, it is amazing that *all* records discovered by the archaeologist thus far which relate to creation *begin* the history of man in a garden, and as a result of direct creation by his god(s). No nations yet have been found with a tradition to the effect that man descended from any of the lower forms of life.

The stories preserved for us on clay tablets speak of (1) the gods creating the heaven and earth; (2) man's origin by the handiwork of god(s), coming direct from god(s), made in his god's likeness; (3) a special day having been set aside after creation; (4) man civilized at his beginning, intelligent and reverent in his ways, without disease and sin, living in a garden appointed by his god(s); (5) trees in the garden for food; (6) peace among animals in this garden; (7) man offending his god(s), resulting in his expulsion from this garden and followed by sin, sickness, misery, and sorrow; and (8) re-entrance into the garden prohibited by sacred images (similar to the cherubim in Gen. 3:24).

102.   Adam and Eve Seal

Although many of these records are corrupted versions of an original tradition and are saturated in polytheism (a belief in many gods), there is a striking resemblance to, and much agreement with, the Genesis record. Stones *are* "crying out" in praise to God and in defense of the inspiration of His Word, especially as they relate to the account of "direct creation."

THE FLOOD

When Solomon said there was no "new thing under the sun" (Eccles. 1:9), he could have had in mind what man *believed* and *did*. No matter how we view the history of man, there is nothing new about his morals. His vices and virtues have not changed since Adam fell. Civilization has advanced man in everything but his morals. We need only to consider the perilous times in which we are living to realize this (II Tim. 3:1-7).

After early man was well established in the "pattern" of civilization as mentioned in the first chapter, "God saw the wickedness of man was great, and that every imagination of his heart was only evil continually" (Gen. 6:5). Though sin abounded, God's grace abounded all the more, and for 120 years Noah, a "preacher of righteousness," warned of judgment to come. Man refused to heed, so the Lord said — "I will destroy man whom I have created from the face of the earth . . . for the earth is full of violence . . . for all flesh had corrupted his way" (Gen. 6:7, 11, 12).

There are at least two reasons why men found it easy to reject Noah's warning. First, truth had no part in their lives, because they had changed "truth into a lie." When man goes this far in changing truth, God's "Spirit will not always strive with man" (Gen. 6:3), and without the Spirit's conviction, no man can turn to God. Secondly, when Noah told the inhabitants that God was going to destroy them with a flood, they mocked him because nothing like that had ever happened before. But God is not to be mocked, and after the ark was completed and those safely inside whom the Lord had called, God sent a "flood of waters upon the earth." The waters prevailed exceedingly upon the earth, all the high hills under the whole heaven

103. Flood Record

were covered, and all, in whose nostrils was the breath of life, died (Gen. 6:17; 7:15-24).

Is the Bible account of the great flood the only record known? There are no less than thirty-three separate racial records among people and races who are living today. Of this number, only the Egyptian and Scandinavian records fail to coincide absolutely with Moses' account. They differ in that their records attribute partial destruction to water and the rest by "direct acts" of many gods. Greek tradition mentions a warning from gods that a great flood would be brought upon the earth because of man's wickedness, that an ark was built, that it rested on a high mountain, and that a dove was sent out twice. "Fa-ha," whom the Chinese say is their founder, is represented as having escaped with his wife, three sons and three daughters from a flood that was sent "because man rebelled against heaven." The English, Hindus, Aztecs of Mexico, Incas of Peru, the Fiji Islanders, and even the American Indians have traditional stories about a flood.

The Polynesian's account of the flood is interesting. In obedience to the commands of the god Kane, Nuu built a large boat with a house on it. Accompanied by his wife and six other people, they rode out the flood in safety. When the flood waters receded, the vessel was on top of Mt. Maunu Kea on the island of Hawaii. He was commanded to leave the ark, and dwell in a cave which he named for his wife, Lili-Noe. This cave remains to this very day. Upon his leaving the ark Nuu offered an animal sacrifice and fruit to his god. Looking at the moon, he thought it was Kane's face, and offered his sacrifice to the moon. This angered Kane, and he came down to punish Nuu. The path over which he came was a rainbow, and when Nuu explained his mistake, Kane went back to heaven over the rainbow, leaving it as a sign of forgiveness.

None can deny that this is a close parallel to the flood events in the Bible. As has been stated, it is generally conceded by ethnologists that when races of people hold to a common, strongly developed belief, there must have been some historical event (or incident) as the basis of that universal tradition. Some of these accounts of the great deluge appear weird and distorted but they testify to at least four Biblical truths: (1) God was offended by man's wickedness; (2) there was an earth-covering flood; (3) there was an ark which saved an obedient man and his family; and (4) there was a new beginning.

Ashurbanipal's library (see p. 67) yielded not only an account of creation, but clay tablets which mentioned the flood. Picture *No. 103* is the "Gilgamesh Epic," which records the Babylonian account of the flood. Gilgamesh was one of the early kings after the flood. This record tells of his search for Utnapishtim (Mesopotamia's Noah) to learn from him the secret of immortality. Utnapishtim relates his "version" of the flood to Gilgamesh, and how he escaped from it. Gilgamesh then pictures himself as the survivor of the flood (*No. 104*). The upper seal shows Gilgamesh and part of his family ready to enter the door of the ark, which resembles a temple door. The lower seal shows two figures in a boat, one standing and the other rowing. To the left, Gilgamesh fights off a human-headed bull or demon, which is attacked also by a lion. He might be trying to keep anyone from getting on board.

Utnapishtim's version of the flood closely parallels the account of Moses — "The gods determined to destroy mankind with a flood, and gave warning. Instructions were given to build an ark and take into it 'the seed of all living

104. Babylonian Noah

things.' The ark was built, a family taken inside and the flood began at an appointed time. Later, the ark came to rest on Mount Nisir, and Utnapishtim sent forth a dove, a swallow, and a raven. The dove and the swallow returned, but the raven saw that the waters were abated and did not return. All left the ark and sacrifices were offered to the gods by Utnapishtim."

The "Gilgmesh Epic" may be gauged by its impact upon other nations. As early as 2000 B.C., it was known in at least four other languages. Its influence on thought and art had spread to other countries and cultures. A fragment found in 1955 at Megiddo reveals that this Epic was known in Palestine in the fourteenth century B.C. By way of comparison, it appears that archaeology's Babylonian account and the Bible's account refer to the same flood.

NOAH'S ARK

Could Noah build a boat big enough to accommodate all that was to be taken inside the ark? Was he "engineer" enough to build such a vessel to withstand its own tremendous weight and size? Critics of the Bible story are amazed when they realize the possibility of such a feat. The instructions and dimensions are recorded in Genesis 6:14-16 — 300 cubits long, 50 cubits wide, and 30 cubits high. When Hezekiah's conduit was discovered (p. 148), an inscription gave its length — 1200 cubits. Measured by our standard, it came to 1800 feet long, making the cubit 18 inches. If this were the length of the cubit of Noah's day the ark was 450 feet long, 75 feet wide, and 45 feet high.

These dimensions are not out of reason when we consider that legendary tales made the ark much larger. One clay tablet tells of a six-story ark with nine compartments in each story. A Grecian account makes the ark 3000 feet long and 12,000 feet wide. Noah's ark, if built with a flat bottom, both ends square and straight up the sides, could offer a carrying capacity of almost 3,000,000 cubit feet. It would take almost 1000 freight cars to provide this much space. The scientific accuracy of Noah's ark is attested to by ships which are built in our present age: six times as long as they are wide.

Noah did not have the problem of finding space in the ark for every specimen and variety of animals and birds. God commanded him to take only of "each kind." Varieties come from a process of "mutation." Noah had only to take a pair of every creature with a pure strain. It was discovered in Mesopotamia not too many years ago that there are about 575 varieties of birds and animals between the size of a field mouse and sheep, and about 290 varieties between the size of sheep and a camel. If half the ark were filled with food, then true species, the number of which Noah took with him, would have occupied an average space of about 170 cubit feet each in the other half of the ark. When we consider that the average size individual takes up about thirteen cubit feet of space, each creature had plenty of room.

MAN'S FAR-REACHING LIFE SPAN

The Sumerian Prism (*No. 105*) was written some one hundred years before Abraham, and is an account of kings who lived prior to and after the flood. The inscription begins with a statement: *"When kingship was lowered from heaven, kingship was [first] in Eridu."* (Eridu is believed by some to be the site of the Garden of Eden.) Then follows a list of eight kings who reigned before the flood. The first two reigned at Eridu, the next three were located in Bar-tibira, which means "city of bronze works," and might be the traditional site of Cain's city (Gen. 4:17). These eight kings ruled a total of

105. Sumerian Prism

241,200 years. The first king, Alulim, ruled for 28,800 years, the second for 36,000, etc. The longest rule was for 43,200 years. This prism gives an exaggerated life-span for the kings who lived before the flood, but their "ageless" life-span is akin to the longevity of the patriarchs who lived in this same era. Adam lived 930 years; Seth, 912; Enoch, 905; Noah, 950; Methuselah, 969; Lamech, 777 (Gen. 5).

Did these men really live this long? Were their years the same as ours? However long it might have been, it is not unreasonable to assume that before the flood man did live a long time. It may be assumed that sin and disease were in their early stages and had only begun their physical effects on mankind. It is reasonable also to assume that man's extended time was necessary in the early period of civilization for him to "replenish" the earth (Gen. 1:28).

At the end of the list of "pre-flood" kings on the Sumerian Prism, there is a summary: *"Then the Flood swept over the earth."* A line is drawn which divides the account of the pre- and post-flood events. Concerning the period after the flood the inscription says: *"When kingship was lowered [again] from heaven, kingship was [first] in Kish."* It then lists seventy-eight rulers of various dynasties in Kish, Ur, Mari, etc. It is noted that the age span of monarchs after the flood decreased, which corresponds to the Biblical record. Abraham's life span was 175 years, Moses' was 120, and subsequently 70 years became the norm (Ps. 90:10).

THE TOWER OF BABEL

The Biblical account of the tower of Babel is but another "myth" — so says the scholarly critic. After Noah and his sons "replenished" the earth (Gen. 9—10), the whole earth was one language and one speech (Gen. 11:1). Post-flood men, failing to give God rightful place, and fearing they might be scattered and lose whatever name they might have or make for themselves, said one to another, "Let *us* make brick, and burn them thoroughly. Let *us* build *us* a city and a tower, whose top may reach unto heaven; and let *us* make *us* a name, lest *we* be scattered abroad." During construction of the city and the tower, the Lord came down to inspect. Finding that nothing now would restrain them doing what they imagined to do, God confounded their tongue, and scattered them abroad. The place was called "Babel" (i.e., "confusion"), because of what the Lord did there (Gen. 11:5-9).

Throughout ancient Mesopotamia numerous towers, called "ziggurats," have been discovered. The great tower at Ur (*No. 106*) measures 200 feet long and 150 feet abroad. The original height is unknown. It was made of burned bricks, which were held together with bitumen. The processional march of worshipers to ascend the tower is illustrated in *No. 107*. Triple stairways led to many upper stages, finally to a throne chair at the top, there to offer sacrifices to the moon-god. The word "ziggurat" means "hill of heaven," which is in line with the Bible's thought of a tower "whose top may reach to heaven." Quite a number of archaeologists believe that the ruins of Marduk's Temple, found inside the city of Babylon, is the real site of the original tower of Babel. A record tells us that the god Marduk gave orders that the temple's "foundations be firm, and its top reach to heaven." The ziggurat at Ur is the best preserved of all the temple-towers discovered, giving to us a good idea what the "Tower of Babel" may have looked like. The stairway of Jacob's dream (Gen. 28:12), and the steps to the altar of Ezekiel's day (Ezek. 43:13-17), are

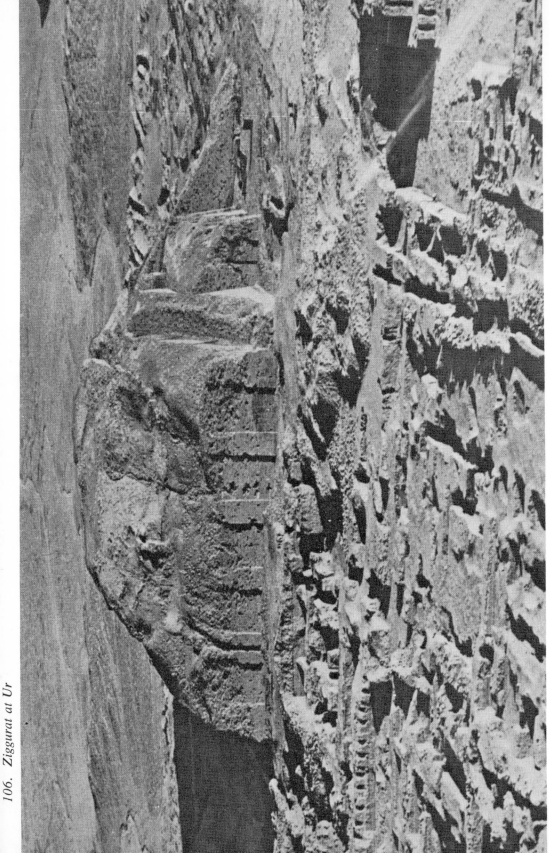

106. Ziggurat at Ur

107. *Restoration of Ziggurat*

somewhat suggestive of the approach to the higher levels of the ziggurat. Discovery of these "towers" reveals to us that man after the flood *did* build "high towers to heaven."

Not only has the discovery of many "ziggurats" helped to confirm the Biblical record of a tower at Babel, but further evidence relates a story of king Ur-Nammu of the Third Dynasty of Ur (2044-2007 B.C.). He received orders from his god and goddess to built the ziggurat (*No. 108*). The stele is nearly five feet across and ten feet high. At the top, the king stands in an attitude of prayer. Above his head is the symbol of the Moon-god Nanna and to the right are figures of angels with vases from which flow the streams of life (the earliest known artistic figures of angels). The panels show the king setting out with compass, pick and trowel, and mortar baskets to begin construction. One panel preserves only a ladder used as the structure was rising. The reverse side records a commemorative feast.

A clay tablet was unearthed which gave the following account of a ziggurat: *"The erection [building] of this tower [temple] highly offended all the gods. In a night they [threw down] what man had built, and impeded their progress. They were scattered abroad, and their speech was strange."* Once again the archaeologist has given to us evidence that the Bible records and accounts of other peoples of other nations are closely related, and that the Bible is not just a "one-sided" account of events and happenings.

While the critics of the Bible still adhere to their theory that Moses "borrowed" all his writings from the accounts of surrounding peoples, the honest and intelligent reader will conclude that accounts of other peoples which have been mentioned convey a "hand-me-down"

version of the Genesis record — *not a source of it.* It is difficult to conceive how Moses could "wash out" the heathen stories of all their myths, superstitions and polytheism and give an account that is purely monotheistic (belief in one God). It is more logical to infer that Genesis gives the original, true record of creation (of the universe and man), sin, the flood, etc. Pagan myths appear later in man's history and seem to be corrupt accounts of the original, even though they contain similarities.

If it is asked why exaggerated, corrupted details and similarities of events recorded in the Bible are found together in secular records, the answer is quite simple. Man, in writing a record of himself, will acknowledge God only insofar as "God" does not interfere with his natural reasoning. To acknowledge God fully is to submit to His authority, admit to a need of Him, and commit one's self to His keeping and care. Such admission places man in a position inferior to God, and this man will not do. Paul said: ". . . when they knew God, they glorified him not as God . . . but became vain in their imaginations as their foolish heart was darkened. Professing themselves to be wise, they became fools. . . . they did not like to retain God in their knowledge . . ." (Rom. 1:21, 22, 28).

As a result of man's rejection of God, we can readily understand why we find additions to, subtractions from, and corruption in the transmissions of a story that puts God above all. We understand better why such "unbelief" has led to a rejection of God, a denial of the "fact" of sin, and the need for a Saviour from sin. Any man who can honestly accept the first four words in the Bible — "In the beginning God" — can accept *all* the Bible as truth, divinely inspired. The believer accepts the Word of God at face value — by faith. He does not need any

108. Stele of Ur-Nammu

evidence to support it, but such evidence as "crying stones" from the pick and spade of the archaeologist will help to refute the denials of God's Word by critics who label its records "myths" or "fable."

In Genesis we have the "book of beginnings." In it is recorded the beginning of everything but God. The great questions of the beginning of heaven, the world, light, vegetation, beasts, man, sin, redemption, prophecy, races and na- tions, languages, arts and science, and the Jew are answered in a simple and rational way. God, having seen man fail utterly three times — by disobedience in Eden, with vain imaginations at the time of the flood, and in confusion at the tower of Babel — now turns to find an upright man who will be a witness to and for Him and who will, as the head of a new nation, be a blessing to all mankind.

CHAPTER 4

Israel—From Abraham to Moses

Genesis 11:26—12:8 gives to us the call of Abraham. When God gave His first prophecy (Gen. 3:15) of a coming Redeemer, His plan was to follow through a long line of successive men until ultimately the "Seed of the woman" (Messiah) would appear (Gal. 4:4, 5). Just as Seth had replaced Abel (Gen. 4:25), and as Noah had been chosen to be God's man in a wicked and adulterous generation (Gen. 6:8), so Abraham is now "recruited" to be the head of a great nation — a man through whom all the nations of the earth would be blessed.

Was there a need for God to again "call out" a man to uphold His name? The building of the Tower of Babel (p. 75) was a result of man's hatred for God — his determination to live without God. At Ur, Abraham's home town, man was again stooping to low levels of sin — worshiping fire, heavenly bodies, the forces of nature, sex, wine, etc. Towers were built to honor gods. Kings were deified and images were made of them for their subjects to worship. Leaving the mountain-peak of monotheism, these men entered the valley of polytheism and established a sad trail of ungodliness. Passionate sex-acts, "sacred" prostitution, sodomy, and many licentious, disgraceful ceremonies between priestesses and male worshipers were the order in Abraham's day. A need to call a man of God's choice *was* in order, and Abraham became that man.

Abraham had not been raised in a home that worshiped the one, true God (Josh. 24:2). His cultural background might lead one logically to assume that his beliefs and ways were those of the peoples of Ur. But God's call indicates otherwise. Within the heart of man the "law of God" is written (Rom. 2:14, 15), and evidently Abraham's heart would not permit a merging of polytheism and monotheism. Ur's environment could not destroy his faith in the true and living God. His continued life of faith and trust in his God throughout his earthly days branded him as "the Friend of God" (James 2:23).

"By faith Abraham, when he was called to go out into a place which he should after receive for an inheritance, obeyed. . . . he sojourned in the land of promise [Canaan], as in a strange country, dwelling in tents" (Heb. 11:8, 9). Abraham's first stop in the land was at Sichem (Shechem; Gen. 12:6, 7), where he built an altar to the Lord. Until the city of Shechem (*No. 109*) was excavated, critics branded its name legend, and that either no city existed in Abraham's day, or the land was not as populated as the Bible states. Archaeological evidence shows that Shechem was one of the many thriving cities in Abraham's day in Canaan. It later became a "City of Refuge" (Josh. 20:7).

Abraham's stay in Canaan was short-lived because of a famine, and he and his wife, Sarah, went down into Egypt (Gen. 12:10). Abraham presented her to the Egyptians as his "sister." A document was discovered in Egypt telling of one of the Pharaoh's who had the husband of a beautiful woman killed that he might have her for his wife. To "protect" himself as well as his wife, Abraham

80

109. Entrance into Shechem

said she was his sister. This was not altogether untrue for Sarah was his half-sister (Gen. 20:12). Abraham ran into this same trouble again when King Abimelech of Gerar took Abraham's wife for himself (Gen. 20).

Archaeology sheds interesting light on Sarah's beauty. She was "a fair woman to look upon" (Gen. 12:11, 14), and a scroll found in a cave near the Dead Sea in 1947 gives us this description of Sarah: *"How fine is the hair of her head, how fair indeed, and her eyes, and how pleasing her nose and all the radiance of her face, how lovely all her whiteness. Her arms goodly to look upon and how perfect her hands. How fair her palms and how long and fine all the fingers of her hands. Her legs how beautiful and without blemish her thighs. All the maidens, and all the brides that go beneath the wedding canopy are not more fair than she. Above all women she is lovely, and higher is her beauty than that of them all, and with her beauty there is much wisdom in her. . . ."* The account goes on to give Abraham's version of how the Egyptian king, Pharaoh Zoan, upon hearing of the beauty of Sarah, *"desired her exceedingly, and he sent at once to bring her to him. He looked upon her and marvelled at all her loveliness, and took her to him to wife."*

God brought judgment upon Pharaoh because of his having taken Sarah, and Abraham and Sarah left Egypt with their possessions, which included gold, silver and livestock. Among the livestock were camels. This might seem unimportant to some, but critics of the Bible long maintained that camels were unknown in Egypt during the time of Abraham. However, drawings, rock carvings, camel bones, and camel images now have been discovered which prove that this animal was domesticated in Egypt long before Abraham's day. Even the minutest details in the Bible are often confirmed by the evidence of archaeology (Gen. 12:14—13:2).

Five Mesopotamian kings invaded Canaan, and kidnapped Lot as they returned home. Abraham pursued the armies of these kings and rescued his nephew (Gen. 14). Critics of Bible history said that the names of these kings were fictional, that in the days of Abraham extensive travel (such as indicated by this military exploit) was unknown and that there was no route east of Palestine. Evidence now shows that the ancient archaic names of these kings are not fictional as claimed by the critic, but are linked with other Babylonian names. A clay tablet from ancient Mesopotamia reveals a contract for a rented vehicle, directing the renter not to drive the wagon as far as the Mediterranian Sea. Further archaeological evidence shows there was a route from Babylon to Canaan, later known as the "King's Highway." The accuracy of Genesis 14 cannot be questioned in the light of such evidence.

Abraham's life in Canaan was influenced to a degree by civil laws which had governed his life while living in Ur. Because he and his wife, Sarah, were childless, it was natural for them to follow a custom of the Sumerians in adopting a son. The purpose was for the son to serve his foster parents during their lifetime, and make provision for their burial after death. This custom might explain why Abraham sought to adopt Eliezer (Gen. 15:2-4).

Sarah was only following a custom of her day when she gave Hagar to Abraham to bear a child. An inscribed contract states that if a wife is childless she shall give a slave girl as a wife to her husband. If the wife were to bear a son later, the son by the slave-wife could not be driven away. This could explain Abraham's reluctance to drive both Hagar and Ishmael out of sight when he was commanded to do so by God (Gen. 16:1-4; 21:9-14).

THE HITTITES

The call of Abraham involved a twofold promise: one was spiritual, that Abraham would be the father of every believer, both of the Old and New Testament eras (Gal. 3:9, 29). The second promise was a natural or material one, that Abraham's seed (through Isaac) would have a land of their own (Gen. 15:18-21). Among the nations residing in this "promised land" was the Hittite kingdom. The people of this nation are mentioned forty-six times in the Word of God, yet critics were bold to declare that "Hittites" never existed, simply because of the absence of any reference to them in ancient literature.

Inscriptions found in Hamath about 1870 made mention of a Hittite people. The Tell el-Amarna letters (No. 169) mention the activities of a Hittite army in Palestine. The letters indicate the Hittite people lived north of Palestine (in Asia Minor). It was not until the early 1900's in Boghazkoy, in central Turkey, that God produced "dead Hittite stones" with living messages. Inscribed material and the ruins of massive stone buildings

110. Hittite Inscription

111. Hittite Divinities

prove beyond a shadow of a doubt that a Hittite empire flourished even before Abraham's day (from about 2100 to 900 B.C.). The kingdom extended from north of the river Euphrates west to the Black Sea in Asia Minor. It formed a worthy third with two other empires of importance — Babylonia-Assyria and Egypt. The Bible mentions the Hittites because there *was* a Hittite nation.

Different styles of Hittite writings have been found, one of which is seen in *No. 110*. There is a cuneiform style, a hieroglyphic style for picture stories, a style for religious purposes, and another for official documents. *No. 111* shows Hittite divinities carved in rock; *No. 112* shows a carving in Egypt of Hittite pris-

112. Hittite Prisoners in Egypt

113. Hittite Royalty in Egypt

114. Stone Door

oners; *No. 113* shows a Hittite king presenting his daughter to Rameses II, a Pharaoh of Egypt. International peace was often kept by exchanging daughters and/or wives.

Hittite discoveries in Turkey and Egypt have served a two-fold purpose. One, they confirmed the Scriptures which relate to the Hittites in Abraham's day. Two, they knocked the props from under the Bible critic who said the land of Egypt was not open to strangers until about 700 B.C. The historian, Diodorus, made this claim, but inscribed accounts of Hittite royalty and prisoners of war in this country, along with other evidence that foreigners were in Egypt as early as 2000 B.C., prove conclusively that Abraham could easily have been there 1300 years before Diodorus' claim. Many times a discovery, while relating to one event, will substantiate the accuracy of another

incident or event recorded in the Scriptures.

MR. LOT — A BACKSLIDER IN SODOM

Lot and Abraham separated because their herdsmen were at odds with each other. Abraham permitted Lot to choose where he would like to settle, and by "sight" Lot pitched his tent toward the wicked city of Sodom (Gen. 13:5-13). Later, he moved into the city (Gen. 14: 12), and, having entered, he lost his testimony. (Read Gen. 19.)

Once Lot had settled in the city, he "sat in the gate of Sodom" (denoting his position as a judge). When two visitors entered the city, Lot entertained them in his own home. The men of Sodom demanded of Lot that he surrender his guests to them — "that we may know them." Lot refused, but offered them his own virgin daughters. The Sodomites ignored this offer and sought to break down the door of his house to lay hold upon the guests. One would think a mob of men could break through a man's door, but probably it was a stone door which was fitted into stone sockets (*No. 114;* see also sockets and door, No. 58). Such a heavy stone door as the one pictured could typify the one in Lot's house. Stone doors were used in stone houses, and usually opened outward. If pushed against by a mob, it was impossible to open or break in, and such a door might explain why Lot's door withstood the pressure exerted by the men of Sodom.

MRS. LOT — A PILLAR OF SALT

A most interesting incident in the Bible is the turning of Lot's wife into a pillar of salt. Because of their much wickedness, God pronounced judgment upon the inhabitants of Sodom and Gomorrah (Gen. 19). He warned Lot saying, "Arise, take thy wife . . . escape for thy life; look not behind thee. . . . Then the Lord rained upon Sodom and upon Gomorrah brimstone and fire from the Lord out of heaven . . . but his wife looked back from behind, and she became a pillar of salt" (vss. 15, 17, 24, 26).

Some time ago an excavation was conducted at Pompeii, Italy, which may shed some very interesting light on the subject of Lot's wife. Pompeii, much like Sodom and Gomorrah, shows mute evidence of vast volcanic deposits. When Pompeii was destroyed in A.D. 79, it did not suffer destruction by hot molten lava, but first, a volcanic gas settled over the city, asphyxiating many of the citizens in their sleep. The city was then covered with heavy deposits of volcanic ash to a depth of about twenty feet, and forgotten — until the archaeologist went to work. The pickmen noticed that their picks struck a hollow place in the ashes. The director gave instructions to the men to open another hole near the first one to act as an air vent. He then pumped plaster of Paris into the "hollow place" and allowed it to dry. After breaking the ashes from around the hardened cast, the director and his staff gazed upon the perfectly "preserved" form of a sleeping woman (*No. 115*). By repeating this method each time a hollow spot was

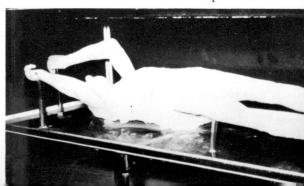

115. Sleeping Beauty

struck, numerous human and animal forms were found (*No. 116*).

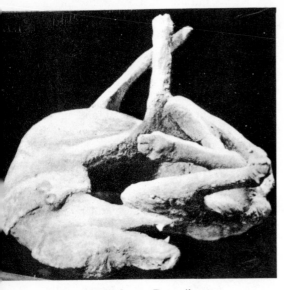

116. *"Roll Over, Rover"*

What happened to cause humans and animals to retain their physical form? The late Harry Rimmer had this to say: "Volcanic ash is heavily impregnated with chemicals, which are water soluble. As time went on, the ash later metamorphosed into a soft stone, somewhat similar to pumice stone. Being porous, water penetrated it freely. The chemical content of the ash worked quickly on the forms of the deceased, and wrought a chemical change which turned their bodies into some chemical, crystalline substance of sufficient hardness to permit the surrounding ash to retain a perfect cast of the buried bodies as it slowly formed into a soft stone. Under the action of water, leaking through the porous rock, the concentration of chemicals which had been a physical form melted, and then disappeared. But the ash-stone matrix retained the shape and features — even the expressions of those dead. After a score of centuries, we are able to look upon the countenances of Pompeii's citizens once again.

"In plain and simple language the recovered 'dead' of Pompeii must have been changed 'into a pillar of salt' of some variety. We use the word 'salt' in its true chemical sense. The term 'pillar of salt' cannot be restricted in its meaning to sodium chloride — common 'table salt,' but must be understood in its broader and fuller sense as a chemical substance. The term 'salt' can be applied to any mineral salt, an iron salt, saltpeter, etc. How long it would take to change a body into any 'salt' is a question whose answer depends upon so many factors we cannot even hazard a guess. It would depend upon the nature of the chemicals present, the amount of heat involved, the degree of pressure applied, and the strength of the solution involved. We can only say that we have at Pompeii the exact conditions which prevailed at Sodom, and clear evidence of the same effect."

Excavations in 1928 in the region of Sodom revealed a stratum of salt 150 feet thick. Over this were large quantities of sulphur, or brimstone. The place was a burned out region of oil and asphalt, where a great rupture in the strata took place centuries ago. Formerly there had been a subterranean lake of oil and gas beneath Sodom. It had been ignited in some mysterious way. A tremendous explosion took place, which carried burning sulphur, oil and asphalt into the air above the cities. Mingled with salt, this brimstone and fire rained down upon the whole plain — just like the Bible says (Gen. 19:24, 25).

The wording concerning Mrs. Lot's becoming a pillar of salt is very interesting. It is stated that she "looked back from behind." She did more than merely stop to see what was taking place. Having left the city with Lot and her daughters, she literally lingered behind — straggled behind the rest. It is quite clear that "back from behind" means that she had deserted the group. Lot had moved so swiftly that he was already in the city of Zoar when the fire and brimstone fell upon Sodom and Gomorrah. Because Mrs. Lot had lingered behind, she evidently was caught in clouds of volcanic gas, and was buried beneath volcanic ashes, just like those at Pompeii. The word "became" is also important. It allows this thought: "In due process of time she became a pillar of salt," or "After a chain of events she eventually was turned, or formed, into a pillar of salt." Regardless of the "how" of her being turned into a pillar of salt, Christ warns us against disobedience by simply saying, "remember Lot's wife" (Luke 17:28-32).

JACOB AND HIS FAMILY

In fulfillment of God's promise to Abraham and Sarah, He gave them a son, Isaac. Although Ishmael was as much Abraham's son as Isaac, Isaac was the "seed of promise" because of his birth through Sarah, who was the "mother of nations" (Gen. 17:15, 16). After Isaac's marriage to Rebekah, twins were born — Esau and Jacob. Esau was the first-born and rightful heir of the Abrahamic promises. But he sold his birthright to Jacob for a "mess of pottage," and what a "mess" this turned out to be. Having been tricked into selling it, Esau vowed to kill Jacob. Unearthed Nuzi tablets (*No. 117*), written in the time of Abraham and Jacob, tell of a man named Tupkitilla, who sold his inheritance rights to his brother for a few sheep.

Jacob, upon learning that his method of obtaining the birthright did not set well with Esau, fled to the home of his uncle Laban in Haran, about four hundred miles northeast of Canaan. Jacob married Laban's daughters — first Leah and then Rachel. Jacob, like Abraham, followed civil customs of the day (as indicated on the Nuzi tablets), and took to himself slave-wives at the request of both Rachel and Leah (Gen. 30:1-4, 9).

When Jacob first became a "part" of Laban's family, it is apparent that Laban

117. Nuzi Tablet

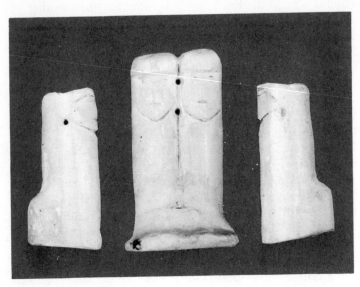

118. "Terraphim" — Family Gods

had no sons of his own, and Laban probably adopted his son-in-law as his son — which would have made Jacob heir of all that Laban possessed. Jacob became indispensable to Laban, but after his father-in-law had his own sons, friction arose (Gen. 31:1). After twenty years in Haran, Jacob and his family left to go back to the "Promised Land." Upon leaving, Rachel stole her father's household gods, or "teraphim" (*No. 118*), and hid them in her camel's "saddle" (Gen. 31:19, 34). Three days after they left, Laban heard of their departure. It took him a week to catch up with them, and his greatest concern was the recovery of his images (Gen. 31:30). Why so much excitement over clay images of gods? Nuzi tablets reveal a law which states that these household gods were the rightful possession of the head of the family. They served as a kind of title deed to all one's possessions. Since Rachel had not forgotten that her father made Jacob work seven extra years for her — and since she knew that her brothers would claim headship over Laban's property, she simply took the gods to "secure" the inheritance for her husband. According to Nuzi law, Jacob could then go before a magistrate with a witness and the family gods and declare ownership (No. 117). This very well explains why Laban was so anxious to recover his "teraphim" (Gen. 31:11-55). He never did find his gods, because Rachel refused to budge from her camel's saddle. Later, Jacob and his household buried these "strange gods" (Gen. 35:1-4). They turned their backs upon any claim to earthly rights, and chose as their priceless heritage a closer walk with the Lord.

JOSEPH IN EGYPT

God prophesied to Abraham that his seed would be "a stranger in a land not their's, and shall serve them and shall be afflicted four hundred years. . . . Afterward shall they come out with great substance" (Gen. 15:13, 14). To fulfill this prophecy, Joseph was chosen by Jacob to receive the birthright. This, coupled with Joseph's dreams and the interpretation thereof, created hatred and jealousy among his brothers. His brothers plotted his life, but later sold him to merchantmen, and Joseph was taken to Egypt. Jacob's son's led their father to believe that Joseph had been killed by a wild beast. In the meantime, and after many events and misfortunes, Joseph was elevated to a position second only to Pharaoh in all the land of Egypt (Gen. 37:1—41:44). Joseph assumed the role of "Secretary of Agriculture" in storing grain during seven years of plenty and its distribution during seven years of famine. "All countries came to Egypt to Joseph to buy corn" (See Gen. 41:45-57). When Jacob heard there was corn in Egypt, he sent his sons to "buy for us that we may live, and die not." In Genesis 42—46 we have the account of the reunion of Joseph and his brothers, and of the moving of Jacob and his family to Egypt, thus bringing to pass the settling of Israel in that land as God's Word had predicted. Located on the west bank of the Nile near Karnak are the ruins of graineries (*No. 119*), said by some to be the site where Joseph met his brothers.

It was not God's "permissive" will that placed Israel in Egypt, but His direct will. ". . . God did send me [Joseph] before you to preserve you. . . . a posterity in the earth, and to save your lives by a great deliverance. So now it was not you

that sent me hither, but God: . . . [and He] hath made me lord of all . . . Egypt: come down unto me . . . and . . . dwell in the land of Goshen . . . thou, and thy children, and thy children's children . . . and all that thou hast; And there I will nourish thee . . ." (Gen. 45:5-11). If Israel were to be the people through whom Messiah was to come, they would have to survive a seven-year famine in which there would be no planting and harvest. God, who foresaw this famine in all the lands, engineered circumstances in such a way that His man was in a land of plenty to save His people from "annihilation by starvation." Seventy souls journeyed to Egypt, and what a "reunion" it was — Jacob with Joseph and Joseph with his whole family. They now had each other — food, shelter, protection, a promise from their God that they would be a great nation, plus assurance that in due process of time they would return to the Promised Land (Gen. 46:3, 4; 50:24).

MUMMIFICATION

Upon the death of Jacob, "Joseph commanded his servants the physicians to

119. Joseph's Graineries

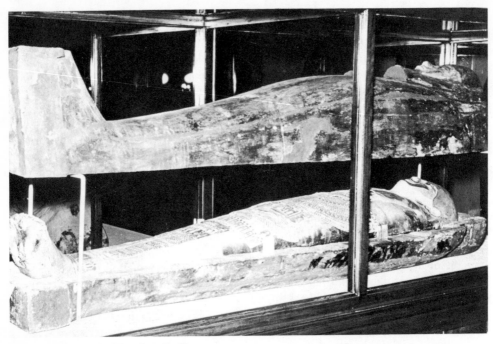

120. Mummy in Wooden Coffin

embalm his father . . . and forty days are fulfilled . . . of those which are embalmed" (Gen. 50:2, 3). Egypt's method of embalming was "mummification," a forty-day (sometimes 70 days) process which preserved (petrified) the body. First, an iron hook was employed to draw out part of the brains through the nostrils, and the rest by infusion of drugs. An incision was then made in the abdomen, removing the internal organs. Having rinsed the abdomen with palm wine, it was then filled with oils, spices and perfumes. The physicians then sewed up the body, and steeped it in natrum for the prescribed number of days. Afterward, the body was washed and wrapped in a flaxen cloth, sometimes as much as six hundred yards, and placed in a coffin. If the coffin was wooden (*No. 120*), it was set upright against the wall. Many times bodies were buried in a sarcophagus (an ornamental stone coffin).

Another method was used in embalming. Syringes filled with cedar oil were injected into the corpse, filling the abdomen. Having prevented the solution from escaping, the body was then steeped in natrum. On the last day the oil was let out from the abdomen, and it had such power that it brought out the intestines and vitals in a state of dissolution. The natrum dissolved the flesh and nothing remained of the body but the skin and bones. *No. 121* shows the mummified head of Pharaoh Setey (Seti).

It is easy to understand how Joseph could make the long journey to Canaan with his father's body in a "mummified" condition (Gen. 50:4-13). Just before Joseph died, he gave instructions for his "bones" (body) to be taken to the Promised Land when Israel left Egypt. When he died, he was "embalmed," placed in a coffin, and "stayed put" for a few centuries till Moses carried out his wishes (Gen. 50:24-26; Exod. 13:19; Josh.

121. *Mummified Head of Setey*

122. Canopic Jar

24:32). The internal organs of the body (heart, lungs, etc.), were removed and placed in "canopic jars" (*No. 122*). The jar pictured here belonged to Tut-ankh-amun (just plain King "Tut" to us). It is about five feet high, and three feet square. Beautifully carved from alabaster stone, it was divided into four receptacles to hold the king's viscera.

ISRAEL IN BONDAGE

For a period of time, the children of Israel enjoyed favor with the Egyptians. Finally, there arose a Pharaoh who knew not Joseph. Because of the number of Israelites and their might, this king set taskmasters over them to afflict them with heavy burdens. The Egyptians made work bitter with hard bondage, in

123. *Egyptian
Water Clock*

mortar, brick, and in their fields. Treasure cities (Pithom and Raamses) were
built by these newly made slaves. The
more they were afflicted the more they
multiplied and grew (Exod. 1:5-14).

An Egyptian "water clock" was used
by "regular" workers (*No. 123*). The
stone cup was filled with water, and em-
ployees stayed on the job as long as the
water dripped from the small opening
(arrow). At the drop of the last drip (or
the drip of the last drop!), work ceased.
Israel in slavery enjoyed no such "luxury"
as a time (water) clock. Taskmasters
(*No. 124*) made life hard for the Israelites. Two slaves are shown trying to
escape from the taskmaster.

It is impossible to say how many of
Egypt's buildings and cities Israel built.
When the cities of Pithom and Raamses
were built, the Israelites were given the
lowest jobs, that of making brick and
mixing mortar. Their labor was all the
more difficult when Pharaoh commanded
straw to be withheld in brickmaking,
thus forcing Israel to go throughout the

124. *Egyptian Taskmaster*

125. Brick with Straw

126. Queen Hatshepsut

land in search of straw and stubble (Exod. 5:6-19). An ancient document found in Egypt, called the "Papyrus Anastasi," relates the complaint of an Egyptian officer, whose duty it was to supervise construction in the land of Goshen. Work had stopped on all projects because "I do not have any materials and help. There is no one to make bricks, there is no straw in this area." The cities of "Pi-tum" (Pithom) and Raamses have both been excavated. Bricks were found that had been made with and without straw. *No. 125* is a brick with straw which bears the name and title of Pharaoh Rameses. The ancient method of brickmaking with straw is still in use today.

THE PHARAOH OF OPPRESSION

It is generally believed that Joseph found favor with a Hyksos king who was then ruling Egypt. After Joseph's death the Hyksos continued to rule until about 1570 B.C. They were defeated, and later expelled from Egypt about 1550 B.C. by Ahmose I of the Eighteenth Dynasty. He was followed by Amen-hotep I (or Amenophis), who was Pharaoh until about 1525 B.C., at which time Moses may have been born. If so, his birth came at the beginning of the reign of Thutmose I. His daughter, Hatshepsut, was probably the princess who found the baby Moses (*No. 126*; Exod. 2:1-10). Moses was later raised in the palace, and was probably identified as an Egyptian until he was forty years old (Acts 7:23).

If Hatshepsut was the princess who found baby Moses, any of the above mentioned Pharaohs could have been the Pharaoh of Oppression. It is quite possible that more than one Pharaoh was labeled by this title. Moses was born in the midst of the oppression — that is why his mother hid him. Let us assume that when Moses was about twenty-one years old Hatshepsut became ruler of Egypt, and was known as the "Female King."

127. Temple of Queen Hatshepsut

128. Hatshepsut's Defaced Images

She ruled from about 1504 until 1482 B.C., and was succeeded by her stepson, Thutmose III, who reigned from 1482 to 1450 B.C. After his death, he was succeeded by his son, Amen-hotep II. To achieve immortality, Hatshepsut built this temple (*No. 127*). She erected inscriptions and images of herself in "contact" with her gods, hoping to leave for all time a record of her piety. Inscriptions proclaimed the god Amun her father by a miraculous conception.

The father of Hatshepsut (Thutmose I) had no sons who could be legal heir. He married his young son of a lesser marriage to his daughter Hatshepsut, and this king became known as Thutmose II. He, too, had no sons who could legally occupy the throne, so he named as his successor a young son and married him to his half-sister, a daughter of Hatshepsut. During his minority Hatshepsut (his step-mother and also his mother in-law) assumed the reign and continued to rule after Thutmose III became of age. When he assumed full leadership, his hatred for the one who had frustrated his ambitions was such that he destroyed her images and defaced her inscriptions (*No. 128*). It is quite possible that Hatshepsut had made mention of Moses on an inscription, but because of his hatred for Hatshepsut and of the Hebrews, mention of any Israelite could have been "erased" from Egypt's picture history.

There are those who contend that Thutmose III was the Pharaoh of Oppression. This hardly seems likely, for it would make Moses forty-three years old when Thutmose III began to reign, and the oppression started before Moses was born. There are some who give a later date for the Oppression and Exodus, making Rameses II (about 1299-1232 B.C.) the Pharaoh of Oppression. There is a difference of opinion among scholars as to Egyptian dates, and it hardly seems likely that "one" Pharaoh of Oppression will be singled out. Suffice it to say, Israel was in Egypt and she was oppressed. (See probable "Pharaoh of the Exodus," p. 108.)

MOSES THE DELIVERER

Moses, the "adopted" son of an Egyptian princess, required a princely education, and was instructed in all the wisdom of the Egyptians (Acts 7:22), who were unsurpassed in civilization by any people in the world. This would fit him for any office in the government, even for the throne. He became familiar with court life, with the military, with their sciences and literature, their law, and with the grandeur and pomp of their religious life. He witnessed the administration of justice (to some) and acquired general acquaintance with the arts of his day. He certainly enjoyed the riches possessed by Egyptian royalty.

EGYPT'S WISDOM

A great part of Egypt's wisdom is seen in her culture and her massive buildings, which reveal her knowledge of several sciences (math and geometry, astronomy, etc.). See "Mathematical Document" (No. 12) and "Medicines," (p. 37). Buildings and monuments erected before Moses' birth (No. 129), during his time (No. 127), and after his death (No. 131), give us insight into Egypt's wisdom.

The Egyptians used wood and brick for their earthly homes, but built their temples and tombs with stone, to last for eternity. The precision with which they erected their structures reveals a "wisdom" that is fantastic. While Hatshepsut's Temple has been called the noblest architectural achievement in Egypt, the Great Pyramid of Khufu, or Cheops (*No. 129*), still stands to this day

129   *The Great Pyramid and Sphinx*

as one of the wonders of the world. Built in about 2600 B.C., it covers thirteen acres, is 486 feet high, and is 764 feet at the base. It took twenty years to complete, contains over 6,000,000 tons of stone (2,300,000 stone blocks average two and one-half tons each in weight). Polished stones on the inside, which made up the king's and queen's chambers, are thirty feet square. They are put together without mortar and are so smooth and closely fitted together that one can hardly tell where they join. It was covered with smooth limestone (over the centuries it has been robbed of this covering for building material and street pavement in and around Cairo). The Great Pyramid is also an astronomical observatory. Its designers knew that the earth is a spheroid, that it rotates on its axis, that it travels on an orbit around the sun, and that the sun travels on its own orbit. In erecting this pyramid, whose corners are almost perfect right angles, the Egyptians had full knowledge that the earth had a ratio of eight inches to the mile in its curvature.

Several Pharaohs erected obelisks, a square shaft with a pyramidal top used as a monumental record of oneself. Quarried from solid granite (*No. 130*), a trough encircled the obelisk. Holes drilled underneath from side to side were inserted with wood. The trough was then filled with water, swelling the wood. This would cause the obelisk to "pop" loose. (This one cracked in the process.) It was then lifted out, smoothed on the bottom side and taken to its place of erection, where the Pharaoh had his record carved on it. Hatshepsut had one, which was covered with gold on the upper third, and probably seen by her "son" Moses. Some obelisks stood as high as one hundred feet.

Rameses II built a Temple (*No. 131*), hewn from a sandstone cliff overlooking the Nile river. In an area about ninety feet square, he caused four colossal statues of himself to be carved, with the royal wife and children represented by small statues at his feet. Between the two middle statues is a door which leads inside the Temple, where rooms have been hollowed out of the rock mountain. The statues of Rameses are sixty-six feet high. In the Temple, known as the Ramesseum, is a colossus of Rameses made of pink granite, weighing one thousand tons.

130. Broken Obelisk

131. *Rameses' Temple — Abu Simbel*

132. *Sacred Cow*

(The statues and Temple have been removed to the mountain's top because rising water from the Aswan Dam covers the area.) Rameses built a Hall at Karnak with 134 gigantic columns (some 169 feet high) with flaring tops, each able to hold a hundred men.

EGYPT'S RELIGIONS

The first kings of Egypt were gods. "Invisible" gods were invented, represented by the kings upon the earth. The god Osiris founded the dynasties of the Pharaohs. He was succeeded by his son Horus, the falcon god. The king was Horus in his lifetime; after death he became Osiris, king over the realm of the dead. By birthright, Pharaoh was a god — "right from the egg" he was king and god and "made conquests while yet in his mother's womb." Although cities as well as states had their gods, Pharaoh was the link between the world and the gods and goddesses. There was cause to rejoice in a royal birth. The gods said, "We created thee"; the goddesses said, "He springs from us."

The main duty of Pharaoh was to ensure the victory of Ma'at, god of truth and justice. Through him the prayers and offerings of the subjects reached the gods. Thanks to him, the gods showered blessings upon the Nile (which in turn was worshiped). He ensured the annual flood of the river, upon which the prosperity of the land depended. He presided over the subsistence of all living things, and (supposedly) vouched for and promoted justice in all social matters. He was the head of the army; nothing could stand in his way. When royal power was weakened, the religions of Egypt broke up, and it was then that sacred animals — fowls, crocodiles, creeping things and insects, spirits and demons — were worshiped. In spite of the fact that multitudes of lesser gods were introduced there was only one Egyptian religion — that of Pharaoh, the god of earth, the unique representative of the faithful before the gods — a god both in life and death — "perpetually venerated in death and perpetually reborn."

Temples contained symbols which represented the earth and heaven. At the foot of the walls were designs of the land of Egypt with vegetable motifs, and a long series of figures in abundance. Above the columns, representing the growth and increase of the land, the ceilings were the vaults of heaven, strewn with blue stars. The pylon in front held religious scenes and rites of the cult, or, more often, pictures of the Pharaoh's victories over all enemies. Temple records have one theme — the triumph of Egypt — thanks to the link of Pharaoh with the gods.

The pyramids were pre-eminently meant to be meeting places of the gods and those of the earth. Their whole conception was designed for a dialog between heaven and earth. Pharaohs who built their pyramids to the sun introduced "Ra" (the sun god) into their own names. One Pharaoh's title was, "Son of the Sun," — "Son of Ra." Statues (colossi and the sphinx) representing Pharaohs, were worshiped, and many of them served as "watch dogs" to keep evil spirits away and would-be robbers from plundering the tombs of the kings.

The religious character of Pharaonic Egypt cannot be stressed too much. Perhaps more than any other ancient civilization, the political, social and economic culture of ancient Egypt rested on a theological basis. It was in this religious setting that the Israelites lived for four hundred years. And Moses lived in this same religious atmosphere with a goddess (Pharaoh's daughter) for forty years. (Egypt was so bound up in its Pharaonic society that its conquerors — Persian, Grecian, then Roman — were obliged to appear as Pharaohs.)

No. 132 is a monument to a "Sacred Cow," one of the many four-footed beasts worshiped by the Egyptians. (See No. 143, similar to the "golden calf" made by Israel in the wilderness. Please read Romans 1:21-25.) *No. 133* is King Tut's throne, with animal representation of one of his gods. His bed and couch also were carved with animal figures, which symbolized his religious beliefs.

133. Throne of King Tut

134. Sacred Pool

No. 134 is a "Sacred Pool." Followers
of the many Egyptian gods believed their
sins could be "washed away" in such
pools. This should not be foreign to us,
for in India today many do the same
thing, including worshiping "sacred" animals. The ancient Egyptians also worshiped birds (No. 124) and snakes (No.
41). No. 135 is a monument to the
"dung beetle," supposedly a descendant
of the goddess of fertility. The eating of
this beetle (alive) by the women was
supposed to produce royalty or deity. No.
136 shows two women facing a dung
beetle in a "birth boat." This act of worship symbolizes their eating it and giving
birth to deity. Figures of beetles also
made up a part of Tut's jewelry (No.
139).

135. Beetle Monument

136. *"Birth Boat"*

Mummification played an important role in the religions of Egypt (see "Mummification," p. 89). This method of embalming was devised to preserve the body for eternity. (Picture No. 121 shows a mummified head.) In re-incarnation, individuals would be part man and part animal or fowl, depending on which "god" was served. The sphinx, which symbolizes one in re-incarnation, has the body of a lion and a man's head. Mummification also enabled the gods to become "human." The goddess Sekhmet became a woman with the face of a lioness. Animals which were deified in this life were mummified for the future life (crocodiles, horses, cows, cats, etc.). The baboon was the god of wisdom. The painting on the wall of King Tut's tomb (No. 136) might indicate that he wanted to be the god of wisdom in eternity. (This is quite a twist from what the "theory" of evolution says in our day, isn't it?) A "soul boat" (*No. 137*) was used to "transport" the soul of the deceased Pharaoh into the presence of Osiris (No. 43).

137. *"Soul Boat"*

EGYPT'S RICHES

When the Bible speaks of the "treasures in Egypt" in Hebrews 11:26, it means riches of untold wealth. The discovery of King "Tut's" tomb in 1922 sheds some light on the fabulous wealth of the Pharaohs and their families. Many tombs have been discovered, but robbers had always preceded the archaeologist. Tut's tomb has been the most elaborate of the Pharaoh's to be found. The outer chamber of his tomb had been plundered, but the sepulchral chamber and treasure room were undisturbed. The Egyptians believed that after-life differed very little from earthly life. A dead king, to attain happiness in the hereafter, had to have food for his body, and provisions for all his wants. When the excavators opened Tut's tomb, which had been untouched for over thirty-one hundred years, they found loaves of bread, jars of meat, water and beer, clothes, jewelry, furniture, chariots, and his throne (No. 133). Found also was his form-fitting coffin which was wrought of solid gold one-eighth of an inch thick, and inlaid with lapis lazuli (*No. 138*). It is over six feet long and weighs more than five hundred pounds. It has a current value of $275,000. The solid gold mask, which covered his head, shows the royal insignia of the vulture and serpent. The face portrays the young Pharaoh. His coffin was inside two wooden cases overlaid with gold, a "rose-granite" sarcophagus, and four shrines (or chapels), the outer one seventeen feet long, eleven feet wide, nine feet high and portable. A linen covering which draped over the framework of the outer chapel, was folded and placed on a stool. This portable chapel with the linen covering could be an ex-

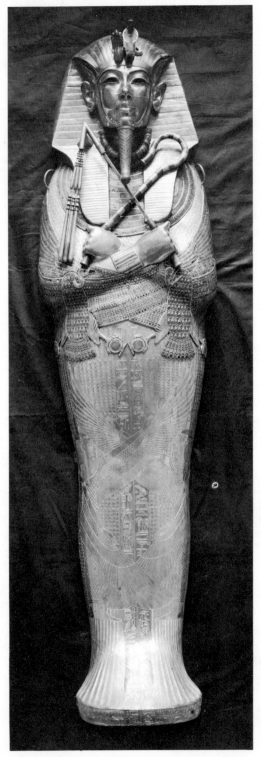

138. King Tut's Coffin

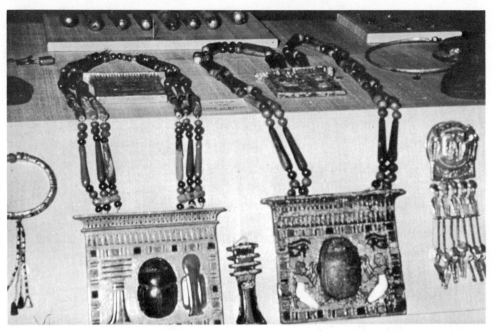

139. King Tut's Jewelry

ample of the "Holy of Holies" and the linen curtains of the tabernacle made by Moses and transported by Israel in the wilderness.

Tut's jewels (*No. 139*) were priceless — gold, silver, and precious stones such as amethyst, lapis lazuli, turquoise and carnelian. Rings and bracelets were wrought with such ingenius and delicate workmanship that even a magnifying glass could not reveal the joints, so perfect was the soldering. His furniture, ceremonial chest, jewel caskets, carrying chair, and clothes chest, which contained his garments of royalty and deity, were overlaid with pure gold. His throne (No. 133), beautifully carved and overlaid with gold and silver, had the image of the king and his wife exquisitely depicted on the back in red glass, carnelian and silver. Within the treasure room he had his gold overlaid chariots in line, "ready" for use. Every part was decorated with embossed design and scenes hammered into the gold, and each was inlaid with

colored glass and stone. A beautiful, ornate alabaster lamp revealed a colored painting of the seated Pharaoh only when its lighted wick was floating in oil.

With his belongings were the royal cartouches, which contained the names of King Tut-ankh-amun, the queen's, Tut's deified name and his emblem. His gold shrines were gilded from top to bottom with artistry of symbols and signs, which were inscribed to "protect" the king's body from those who would rob and steal, and from the touch of time itself. One of Egypt's finest carvings of precious stone, a model of Tut's funeral boat in alabaster, was also found (*No. 140*). Life-size figurines, made of bituminized wood and decorated with beaten gold, stood at the entrance chamber as guards against tomb plunderers. On the door was a carved headless demon, guardian of all the Pharaoh possessed for the life to come.

Although Moses was schooled in all the wisdom and the religions of the

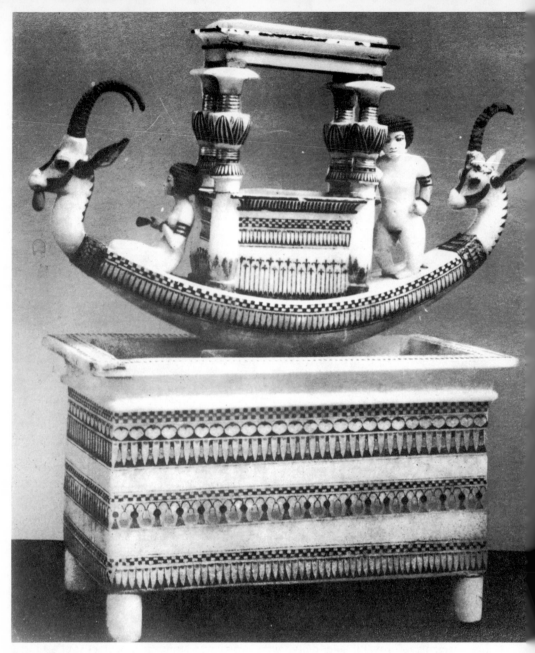

140. *Model of Funeral Boat*

Egyptians, mighty in words in the kingdom as the queen's "son," mighty in military deeds as an Egyptian officer (which prepared him for leading Israel), and, in spite of the fact that possibly under the queen he might have become a Pharoah and a "god," plus being a multi-millionaire as a member of the royal family, he "refused to be called the son of Pharoah's daughter . . . esteeming the reproach of Christ greater riches than the treasures in Egypt . . ." (Heb. 11:24, 26). What a tremendous help the archaeologist has been to us in revealing what Moses forsook in casting his lot with God and Christ. We sometimes forget that people in Old Testament days were just as human as we, and that they, too, were confronted with decisions for God. To be with God and His people was far more important to Moses than all Egypt's wealth. To forsake such fame and wealth might be a hard decision for many, but not for one with "eternity's values in view," such as Moses. "What shall it profit a man if he shall gain the whole world, and then lose his own soul?" (Mark 8:36).

Following one assumption, Hatshepsut was on the throne when Moses made his decision. With full recognition that he was still a Hebrew by birth, he sought to aid two of his brethren. In so doing he killed an Egyptian and incurred the wrath of Pharaoh. Moses fled to the land of Midian, there to dwell on the far side of the desert for the next forty years. While he was there, the Israelites in bondage cried to God for relief, and Moses was raised up to deliver them. With Aaron, his brother, he mapped the strategy to take Israel out of Egypt and bondage (Exod. 2:11—4:31).

THE EXODUS

"Moses and Aaron went in, and told Pharaoh, thus saith the Lord God of Israel, Let my people go . . ." (Exod. 5:1). Instead of releasing Israel, Pharaoh made their work all the harder. Because Pharaoh defied God, the Lord said, "Now shalt thou see what I will do to Pharaoh: for with a strong hand shall he let them go, and . . . drive them out of his land" (Exod. 6:1).

THE TEN PLAGUES

Because of the "hardness" of Pharaoh's heart it took ten "plagues" to bring the king to his knees before the Lord. Since all Pharaohs claimed deity, it is easy to understand why Pharaoh asked Moses, "Who is the Lord, that I should obey his voice to let Israel go?" (Exod. 5:2). The request was immediately denied. Then God did a most unusual thing. "The Lord said to Moses, See, I have made thee a god to Pharaoh" (Exod. 7:1). Pharaoh now had competition. It was god versus god — God versus god. Then God sent Moses before the king again, saying, "Speak all that I command thee . . . unto Pharaoh, that he send the children of Israel out of his land. And I will . . . multiply my signs and wonders in the land of Egypt" (Exod. 7:1-3).

These signs and wonders were in the form of plagues or judgments upon Pharaoh, his people, and his land. They were designed to exhibit the powerlessness of Egypt's gods. In each of them, God revealed His superiority to both the Egyptians and Israel, "that ye shall know that I am the Lord your God" (Exod. 6:7). Archaeological evidence reveals that each plague was a "strike" at an Egyptian god. The turning of the Nile into blood exposed the helplessness of this "god" to give its worshipers a satisfactory flood to fertilize the land. A sudden increase in the number of animals and insects (who were considered deities), and disease and death upon them, was God's way of showing Egypt how helpless their gods were to deliver themselves. There were gods of nature, but hail and extended darkness proved that the God of Israel was Master over nature. When boils afflicted the Egyptians, even the beasts which were worshiped could not help their subjects. Although Pharaoh came to the realization that the God of Israel was the true and living God, it took the death of the firstborn, who was supposed to be a "fullblooded" god by birth, to make him yield to God's demands that Israel be granted permission to leave (Exod. 7:14—12:32).

THE PHARAOH OF THE EXODUS

Solomon began to reign about 970 B.C. During the fourth year of his reign, 480 years had lapsed since the Exodus (I Kings 6:1). The fourth year of his reign would be 967 B.C., and thus the Exodus would be dated about 1448 B.C., putting it in the reign of Amen-hotep II (*No. 141*), who began to reign in 1450 B.C. He, then, in all probability, was the Pharaoh of the Exodus, the Pharaoh before whom Moses appeared at the age of eighty (Exod. 7:7).

Having been granted permission to leave Egypt, Israel gathered her meager belongings, borrowed of the Egyptians jewels of silver and gold and began her exodus (Exod. 12:29-37). When the Israelites were on their way out, Pharaoh changed his mind, and in swift chariots his army pursued them toward the Red Sea (*No. 142*). But the die was cast for Israel, and God's miracle of opening the Red Sea delivered her but destroyed Pharaoh's army (Exod. 14:5-31).

THE WILDERNESS JOURNEY

In the third month after leaving Egypt, Israel camped before Mount Sinai, where God gave Moses the "Decalogue" (Ten Commandments) and other laws to govern the nation (Exod. 19—32). While Moses was receiving the Law, the people persuaded Aaron to help make a "god" for worship. It was made in the form of a calf from the gold earrings which the Egyptians had given them. It probably represented the Apis bull calf (*No. 143*). When Moses learned of this, his anger was kindled and he broke the "tables of stone" containing the Law. Because of Israel's sin of idolatry, three thousand men lost their lives (Exod. 32).

After atonement was made for this sin, God gave Moses a second table of the Law (Exod. 34). Instructions for the

141. Amen-hotep II

142 Egyptian Chariot

building of the Tabernacle had been given when Moses first went up on Mount Sinai. So often we make Sinai the symbol or type of the Law. However, having received plans for the Tabernacle also, which is a type of Christ, Sinai becomes a type of "law and grace" — the Law being the schoolmaster which leads to Christ (Gal. 3:24).

Much of the metal used in the construction of the Tabernacle came from the jewelry given by the Egyptians to the Israelites. The women gave up their rings, bracelets and their "lookingglasses" (Exod. 35:22-29; 38:8). Since glass was not used in the Tabernacle, this reference is puzzling. Archaeologists give us the answer — "lookingglasses" in our King James Version were mirrors made of copper, and finely polished (*Nos. 144, 145*).

No. 146 is an ivory fragment depicting a cherubim, and could well depict the Tabernacle cherubim. The cherubim was woven in the fine linen of the Holy of Holies, and made for the "Mercy Seat," which was the lid of the Ark of the Cove-

143. Apis Bull Calf

144. Copper Mirrors

145. Madame Egypt's Beauty Salon

nant (Exod. 25:20; 37:7-9. See p. 104 for possible description of the Holy of Holies, and No. 172 for Ark of the Covenant.).

After the Israelites left Horeb, they journeyed in the wilderness to Kadesh-barnea, an eleven-day journey (Deut. 1: 2). The spies' report of well-fortified cities in Canaan caused Israel's faith to

146. Cherubim

147. Fortified Canaanite City

148. *Siq—Petra's Entrance*

149. View of
Petra's "Buildings"

melt, and she turned back into the wilderness, there to roam for an additional thirty-eight years before entering the Land of Promise (Num. 13:1—14:39). These strongly fortified cities of Canaan (*No. 147*) struck terror into the hearts of Israel (Num. 13:27, 28).

Leaving Kadesh-barnea, Moses sought passage through the mountains of Seir, the land of the Edomites (Num. 20:14-17). One of the cities in Seir was Selah (now called "Petra, the Red-Rose City, Half as Old as Time"). Completely surrounded by rock mountains, its only entrance is a narrow gorge called the "Siq" (sick), which is just about two miles long (*No. 148*).

Jeremiah spoke of the Edomites as "Thou that dwellest in the clefts of the rocks, that holdest the height of the hill" (Jer. 49:16). The land of Seir is one of the most rugged places on earth. To get to Petra, one must either walk or ride horseback. We rode. Once inside the city, the colors are awe inspiring, ranging from light to dark, yellow to brown, red to purple, and from white to pastel shades. The "buildings" are facings hewn from the rocky mountain sides (*No. 149*), with countless rooms hollowed out. There are banquet halls, government buildings, palaces, temples, monasteries, tombs, shops, and houses. Each conqueror "faced" buildings in their own architectural style. Petra today is of Nabatean style. Carved rock steps, leading past temples, ascend to the highest mountain peak, or "high place," carved to offer humans as sacrifices and worship graven images (*No. 150*). Probably at

150. Petra's High Place

151. *Treasury Building at Petra*

this "high place" King Amaziah took ten thousand Edomite captives and cast them down from the top of the rock (II Kings 14:1-7; II Chron. 25:11, 12). *No. 151* is a close-up of Petra's "Treasury" building.

The Israelites were refused passage through the land of the Edomites (Num. 20:18-21). Moses sought to lead the Israelites over the "route of the spies," but King Arad fought against them. No matter where Moses sought to go through Seir to Moab, he was rebuffed. Discoveries have revealed the ruins of many fortified cities in the valley adjacent to the mountains of Seir (small dots on the map indicate these cities; No. 153). It was because of these fortified positions that Moses had to lead Israel ". . . by way of the Red Sea [Gulf of Aqaba], to compass the land of Edom" (Num. 21: 4). What a "long way around" one must go when God's way is refused.

It is said of Israel that she was "set to mischief" (Exod. 32:22). How true this was of her wilderness journey! After crossing the Red Sea, she became a "typical" Christian — a complainer. She complained about her leaders (Exod. 15:24; Num. 16:3; 21:5); water (Exod. 15:24; Num. 20:2-11); Moses' absence, which resulted in making the golden calf (Exod. 32:1); the desert (Exod. 16:1, 2; Num. 20:2-5); food and meat (Exod. 16:2, 3; Num. 11:4-6, 18-20, 31-33; 21:5); inhabitants of other nations (Num. 13:31; 14:2); God's judgments (Num. 16:41); and having to encompass the land (Num. 21:4).

It is no wonder that Moses called the children of Israel "rebels" (Num. 20:10). His patience was exhausted because they were fickle, but God's was not, for He remembered His covenant promises to His people. As Israel approached the land of Moab, they were refused permission by the king (*No. 152*) to pass through

152. Amorite King

Amorite territory. God enabled Israel to smite the Amorites, and she possessed the land of Moab east of the Dead Sea (Num. 21:11-31). With a need to advance farther northward before they could enter the Promised Land, they went up by way of Bashan and defeated King Og at Edrei. This victory enabled Israel to possess the land east of the Jordan river as far north as Mt. Hermon (Num.

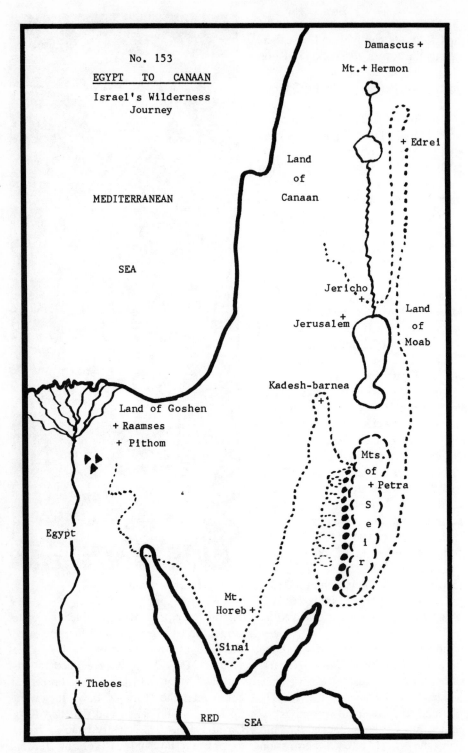

No. 153

EGYPT   TO   CANAAN

Israel's Wilderness
Journey

MEDITERRANEAN

SEA

Damascus +

Mt. + Hermon

+ Edrei

Land
of
Canaan

Jericho
+.

Jerusalem
+

Land
of
Moab

Kadesh-barnea
+

Land of Goshen
+ Raamses
+ Pithom

Mts.
of
+ Petra
S
e
i
r

Egypt

Mt.
Horeb +

Sinai

+ Thebes

RED   SEA

153. Egypt to Canaan

21:32-35; Deut. 4:45-49). Israel then encamped in Moab, opposite Jericho at the Jordan river (Num. 22:1: See Map, *No. 153.*).

WARNINGS AGAINST IDOLATRY IN CANAAN

In the meantime, God gave Israel certain instructions and warnings about the inhabitants of the land of Canaan — their idolatry and their sins in the worshiping of Baal. "After the doings of the land of Canaan, whither I bring you, shall ye not do; neither shall ye walk in their ordinances" (Lev. 18:3). Archaeological discoveries reveal Baalism to be a religion of immorality — vice and sex — in which children were offered as human sacrifices to the god Baal. Texts (*No. 154*), found at the ancient Canaanite city of Ugarit (now called Ras Shamra, in northern Syria), give us the mythological background of this religion, which was common in the days of Lot and during Israel's tenure in Canaan.

154. Ras Shamra Tablet

156. God of Harvest

155. Baal

157. *God of Storm*

158. *God of War*

159. *Temple at High Place*

BAAL WORSHIP

To the Canaanites, Baal alone was *the* god (*No. 155*). He was the god of nature — rain, sun, harvest, and storm (*Nos. 156, 157*). He alone had the power of rain to quench the dry land and give harvest. He alone had control over water and storm. He alone was the god of war to give his subjects victory over their enemies (*No. 158*). In spite of the fact that Baal was supposed to be their god for all these things, he was powerless when Israel's God rolled back the waters of the Jordan river for them to cross over dryshod (Josh. 4:18-24). Baal could not aid the Canaanites when they fought against Israel at Ajalon. More of Baal's followers were killed in the storm of hail stones than died by the sword (Josh. 10:11). Perhaps the most dramatic "struggle" between the God of Israel and the god Baal is found recorded in I Kings 17—19. Because of Israel's sin of worshiping Baal, rain was withheld in the land, and a severe drought and famine followed. The "contest" on Mount Carmel was to decide which deity was the "lord of nature." Baal, represented by 450 prophets, failed to "make it rain." God, represented by just one of His servants, succeeded (I Kings 18:17-39).

The followers of Baal erected temples (*No. 159*) and altars (*No. 160*) on hilltops or "high places" near their villages where they offered sacrifices and performed their rites. They offered their children as human sacrifices (*No. 161*), as well as burnt-offering sacrifices to Baal.

160. Altar

161. Human Sacrifice

162. *Incense Stands and Prayer Beads*

163. *Stone Serpent*

They also worshiped demons (Deut. 32: 17; see No. 42), used idols, incense stands and prayer beads in their rituals (*No. 162*), and paid homage to serpents (*No. 163*) and to creeping things. Baal was also the "god of sex" (*No. 164*). His mother, Asherah (translated "grove" in the K.J.V.), was the patron goddess of sex (*No. 165*). The hillsides (or high places) were dotted with "groves" (or Asherim), which were handcarved, sex-cult objects — tree stumps on each side of an altar — one conspicously displaying the privates of a man and the other exhibiting in like manner the sex organs of a woman. Baal's sister and mistress, Anat, engaged Baal in sexual relations, thus causing the worshipers of Baal to promote fertility in "sacred sex acts." As the religious leaders of Baalism publicly practiced immoral sex acts, the people of Canaan gave vent to their lustful passions, and adultery became the norm in the land. In one scene Baal had sexual intercourse with a heifer. Before they entered the land God had warned Israel against the awful sins of adultery, homosexuality, bestiality, and the offering of their children as human sacrifices (Lev. 18:3-30).

165. Asherah

164. God of Sex

Canaan's sins were most heinous. They all revealed a polytheism which was grotesque and vile. Probably human sacrifices, homosexuality and bestiality were the worst features. Baalism was an utterly depraved religion. It is no wonder that God commanded Israel to "utterly destroy" the nations in Canaan, to show no mercy upon them, to break down their altars and images and burn them with fire, to make no covenant with any of them, and not to marry any of them (Deut. 7:1-5). If Israel failed to obey this command, she would soon mingle with the people, and become a part of their sins (Deut. 20:17, 18). It is a wonder that God did not destroy the Canaanites sooner.*

COULD MOSES HAVE WRITTEN THE PENTATEUCH?

Our answer to this question is Yes, for "holy men of God spoke as they were moved by the Holy Spirit" (II Peter 1: 21). Christ Himself believed Moses' writings (Luke 16:31; 24:27, 44). But the critics of the Bible said No — that man was too primitive in Moses' day, and that his laws were too advanced for his times (about 1500 B.C.). The Code of Hammurabi (*No. 166*), which was discovered in 1902 and written several centuries before Moses' day, proves that moral laws were known long before Moses wrote the Pentateuch. With this defeat, the critics then accused Moses of copying Hammurabi's laws. For a long time they appeared to be successful, but after a comparison of these two sets of laws, it was discovered that Hammurabi, under the approval of the sun-god Shamash, permitted immorality, as well as other sins, to be practiced. The Mosaic Law, far superior to Hammurabi's, condemns the practice of sin, thus showing that the Hebrew laws dealing with morality and holiness were not derived from the Babylonians as the critic would have us believe (See pp. 25, 66).

166. Code of Hammurabi

---

*For a detailed study of Baalism, see the author's book — *Baal Worship in Old Testament Days*.

CHAPTER FIVE

Israel—In and Out
and Back Into the Land

The government of the children of Israel rested upon Joshua after the death of Moses. He led them over the Jordan river into the "Promised Land," that they might "possess their prossessions." The first city to be conquered was Jericho (*No. 167*), whose walls came "a tumblin" down in obedience to God's instructions (Josh. 6). Jericho was excavated in the early thirties by John Garstang, who found the fallen walls of Joshua's day. He states that the wall had fallen down the slope in a manner that permitted the invaders to crawl into the city. Critics have raised some objections to the "Jericho story" of the Bible. First, they argue that "engines of war" (Ezek. 26:9, No. 20) would have forced the city's walls "inward," while the Biblical account states the wall "fell flat." Archaeological evidence by Garstang proved them wrong. Secondly, they argued that materials used in ancient buildings, such as stones and mud bricks with straw, could not burn. They forget that other materials were also used. Even in our day some of our "fireproof" buildings have burned. Ash layers found by Garstang indicated a holocaust, just as the Bible recorded: "And they burnt the city with fire . . ." (No. 60). Thirdly, they argue that "if" the wall did fall, Rahab's house would have been destroyed, and Scripture indicates hers was not. Garstang found that Jericho was bounded by an outer and inner wall, and portions of the inner wall were still standing. Evidence revealed that houses were built on top of the inner wall. (See p. 66.)

God pronounced a curse upon the man who would rebuild Jericho, saying that "he shall lay the foundation in his firstborn [son], and in his youngest son shall he set up the gates of it" (Josh. 6:26). Just as we use a "cornerstone" when dedicating a building, the custom in ancient days was to sacrifice a child in erecting a building or a city wall (No. 161). Hiel the Bethelite rebuilt Jericho, and offered his two sons as sacrifices (I Kings 16:34). Recent excavations at Jericho trace the city's history to the earliest of times. While some question the interpretation of Garstang's findings, no occupational level has been discovered between the Jericho of Joshua's day and the Jericho Hiel rebuilt in King Ahab's day.

Israel was defeated in her next battle at Ai, but was able to defeat this city in the second battle (Josh. 7—8). Moving toward the city of Gibeon (Josh. 9:1—10:15), Joshua found himself tricked by the men of Gibeon. In spite of God's command not to "join" with any of the inhabitants of the land, God gave them victory. The men of Gibeon were punished by being made "hewers of wood and water carriers" (Josh. 9:22-27). Such punishment might seem mild to us, but in the East it is the woman's job to carry water, not man's. How humiliating this must have been to these men!

Recent discoveries at Gibeon by James B. Pritchard show that this city had one of the most extensive water systems ever unearthed in Palestine. Tunnels were hewn out of solid rock a distance of 389 feet, with more than 172 steps for "water carriers" to have easy access to the pools or cisterns. This city was widely known for its water supply (Jer. 41:12). The men of Joab and the men of Abner

167. *Fallen Walls of Ancient Jericho*

fought a battle at one of Gibeon's pools (*No. 168*; II Sam. 2:12-17). Johanan found Ishmael, the "usurper, by the great waters that are in Gibeon" (Jer. 41:11, 12). How did Dr. Pritchard know that this buried city was Gibeon? He found a short Hebrew inscription on the handle of a jar which said, "Gibeon." An inscribed piece of pottery listed the name of "Hananiah," a name given to the son of Azur, the prophet "who was of Gibeon" (Jer. 28:1). During another season additional inscriptions were found, not only with the name "Gibeon," but with actual names of Gibeon's prominent citizens. Some were Biblical names — Azariah, Amariah, Nahum, and Meshullam.

Joshua continued to lead Israel throughout the land. They conquered one city after another, until they "took

168. Pool of Gibeon

169. Tell el-Amarna Tablets

the whole land, according to all the Lord said unto Moses" (Josh. 10:28—11:23). One reason why the Israelites met with such success in taking the Promised Land was God's having "sent the hornet" before them, which drove them out from before them, even the two kings of the Amorites (Exod. 23:28; Deut. 7:20; Josh. 24:12). While Israel was in the last years of her Egyptian bondage, Thutmose III and his successor waged a series of military invasions in Canaan, overcoming their defenses and conquering the people. Archaeologists have discovered that Thutmose III had as his personal badge, "The Hornet," which, in all probability, referred to him and his "Hornet Army."

In 1887 a peasant woman found some clay tablets along the Nile river at Tell el-Amarna, which sheds much light on Israel's conquest of Canaan (*No. 169*). Many of these tablets were letters written by the kings of Canaan and Syria to Egyptian Pharaohs, asking help against warriors invading their lands. One invading group east of Jordan was called

"Habiri," known as the Israelites, or Hebrews.

Merneptah ruled in Egypt about 1224 to 1214 B.C., and was forced to defend his empire against invading people from the North. In the record of his campaign in Palestine (*No. 170*), he mentions different Sea Peoples, among them Israel in Canaan. This monument provides the

170. Merneptah ("Israel") Stele

first mention of Israel in Egyptian records, and is proof that Israel was in Palestine by 1220 B.C. The word "Israel" (enlarged line) is designated as a "people" and suggests that they were not yet regarded as a settled political unit or "nation," as they were known when Saul became king.

The question is often asked, "Did Israel possess all the land which God promised?" The Bible answers: "Joshua took the whole land . . . , and . . . gave it for an inheritance unto Israel according to their division by their tribes. . . . The Lord gave unto Israel all the land that he sware to give unto their fathers; and they possessed it and dwelt therein. . . . There failed not ought of any good thing the Lord had spoken unto the house of Israel; *all came to pass*" (Josh. 11:23; 21: 43-45). The original promise to Abraham included the land from the "river of Egypt to the river Euphrates" (Gen.

15:18). King David's dominion was established by the river Euphrates (I Chron. 18:3). Solomon's was to the border of Egypt (II Chron. 9:26). Lest someone might say this does not mean "the river of Egypt," we need only refer to his feast celebration "unto the river of Egypt" (II Chron. 7:8). Solomon testified that "there had not failed one word of all his good promises," which God had promised to Israel concerning the land (I Kings 8:56). Nehemiah, when reveiwing the faithfulness of God and Israel's rebellion, said "the children went in, and possessed the land" (Neh. 9:23-25). It appears from the Scriptures that Israel *did* possess *all* of her land.

However, Israel *failed* to "drive out" all the inhabitants as God had commanded. A new weapon — "chariots of iron" (*No. 171*) — posed a new threat to them, and the inhabitants of the valley were not defeated (Judg. 1:19). Al-

171. Iron Chariot

172. Ark of the Covenant

though Israel's victory in the land was incomplete, she became strong and "taxed" the Canaanites (Judg. 1:28). Having settled in the land, Israel set up the Tabernacle at Shiloh. The Ark of the Covenant (*No. 172*), which had been set in its proper place "between the cherubims" (No. 146), was later taken out of the Tabernacle and was captured by the Philistines (Josh. 18:1; I Sam. 4:1-11).

ISRAEL'S UNITED KINGDOM

It was due to God's promise that Israel got the land, but she "waxed fat" as Moses predicted (Deut. 31:20), and fell easy prey to her enemies. The book of Judges gives us an account of their lives, actions and offices of the Judges whom God raised up to deliver Israel. This book records seven times that Israel did evil in God's sight. It ends with every man doing that which was right in his own eyes (Judg. 21:25). Forgetting that God had chosen her to be a "pattern" to other nations — to do what was right in *His* eye — Israel demanded "a king over us, that we also may be like all the nations" (I Sam. 8:1-20).

Samuel pleaded with the people to keep God enthroned, but they "dethroned" Him, making Saul their king (I Sam. 9:1—10:1). He was a selfish, wayward, jealous king, and unfaithful to his allegience to God (I Sam. 9—31). Saul was temperamental, and David often soothed the king's nerves by playing the harp (*No. 173*; I Sam. 16:23). Once when Saul was in a fit of anger, David hid in a cave of Adullam (*No. 174*), which is located in the Judean wilderness between Bethlehem and the Dead Sea (I Sam. 22:1). *No. 175* is a carving of a Philistine soldier with a helmet, which depicts the giant Goliath, whom David slew (II Sam. 17).

173. *Cave of Adullam* 174. *"David's" Harp*

175. *Goliath's Helmet* 176. *Tear Bottles*

Saul's life came to a bitter end. After his death the Philistines stripped him of his armor, and placed it in the house of the fertility goddess, Ashtaroth. They took his head and placed it in the temple of Dagon (I Sam. 31:6-10; I Chron. 10: 1-10). The Old Testament site of Bethshan has been excavated, and the house of Ashtaroth and the temple of Dagon have been discovered — believed to be the ones where Saul's armor and his head were placed.

David was Israel's next king. Chosen by God, he was a man after God's own heart, a great soldier, a champion as well as a courageous king (I Sam. 16: 1-13; Acts 13:22; I Sam. 17:34-40; II Sam. 5:7). He was also a man of passion and experienced deep grief and sorrow as a result of his sins. When Saul sinned, he blamed the people (I Sam. 15:1-30). When David sinned, he acknowledged it before God and sought forgiveness (II Sam. 12:13; Ps. 51). In Psalm 56:8 he mentions his tears being placed in a bottle. An ancient custom during the time of heartaches and sorrows was for people to hold their "tear bottles"

177. *"Cup" of the 23rd Psalm*

beneath their eyes to catch their tears of grief. These bottles were sealed and kept in a conspicuous place in the home. Upon death, these bottles were buried with the owner as one of his most sacred possessions. Made of thin glass, they vary in size, from three to six inches in height (*No. 176*). When David said "my sin is ever before me" (Ps. 51:3), he could quite possibly have been referring to the tears of repentance in his tear bottles.

In all of David's heartbreaking experiences, his trust in God was deepened. So complete was his trust that he said, "The Lord is my shepherd, I shall not want. . . . My cup runneth over" (Ps. 23). David knew what it was to be a shepherd, to lead a flock by springs or wells and fill stone basins or "cups" (*No. 177*) to overflowing. He used this as an illustration to reveal God's goodness and mercy.

Although God's blessing was upon David, he had to reap what he had sown in adultery and murder. The son conceived by the woman out of wedlock died, and left him brokenhearted (II Sam. 12:1-23). His daughter was raped by his son (II Sam. 13:1-22). Absalom, the son whom David loved dearly, won favor with the people and David had to flee for his life from the army of Absalom. The division between father and son culminated in a battle, and Absalom died as a result of hanging (II Sam. 15—19). "Absalom's Pillar" is the traditional name given to this monument (*No. 178*). (See II Sam. 18:18.)

Solomon was the third and last king of the "United Kingdom" of Israel. He was known as the king "of wisdom and folly." His wisdom came as a result of his desire to be a good king (I Kings 3:5-28). His downfall came as a result of his desire for "strange women," who turned him from the Lord to "strange gods" (I Kings 11:1-25).

Solomon was a builder. Most notable of all his buildings was the Temple at Jerusalem, which replaced the old Tabernacle (*No. 179*). The quarry from which the stones of the Temple were cut is beneath Jerusalem (*Nos. 180, 181*). Some blocks of stone used in the Temple make up the lower part of the old "Jewish Wailing Wall" (*No.* 182). In I Chronicles 22:14 and 29:4, 7 we have a list of the vast store of material for the Temple with an approximate value of almost $5,000,000,000. The city of Megiddo was one of Solomon's cities, constructed in all probability for his cavalry (I Kings 9:15-19). It is estimated that the extensive stables at Megiddo could hold up to five hundred of his forty thousand horses (I Kings 4:26). Some of the "hitching posts" were discovered at this ancient site (*No. 183*). Another city Solomon built was Gezer. Found there was the "Gezer Calendar" (*No. 184*), which gives instructions for agricultural activities of the twelve months. As the earliest known Hebrew inscription, it is of interest in that it provides a relatively fixed date to help in the study of the development of the Hebrew language. King Solomon also built pools (Eccles. 2:6) to bring water into the city of Jerusalem (*No. 185*). A few years ago construction workers built a new road from Jerusalem to Bethlehem and unearthed a conduit of Solomon's day (*No. 186*). The Romans had also built a conduit (upper) to utilize the water from Solomon's pools. Had they gone a foot lower they could have used Solomon's! There is a span of approximately nine hundred years between the two.

In Solomon's greatness he built his own beautiful palace and the Temple. But his love of luxury and excessive building brought about forced labor and higher taxes. He multiplied to himself horses (I

178. Absalom's Pillar

Kings 4:26; 10:28, 29), wives (I Kings 11:1-3), and gold and silver (II Chron. 9:13-28) in open violation of the command of God (Deut. 17:14-20). The gold utensils give an idea how some of Solomon's vessels looked (*No. 187*). He accumulated such an abundance of gold that his ivory throne was overlaid with gold, his footstool was gold, all his drinking vessels and the vessels of his house were pure gold (none were of silver), and his soldiers used shields of gold. Silver was so plentiful in his day that it was as common as the stones on the hillsides. Solomon even built a seaport on the Red Sea (Aqaba Gulf) and a navy to import these metals, much of which came from Ophir (I Kings 9:26-28). David himself had three thousand talents of Ophir gold for the Temple (plus other talents of gold as well; I Chron. 29:4; 22:14. A talent of gold was worth around $30,000.). An inscribed piece of pottery mentions Ophir gold (*No. 188*). This, along with an inscribed stamp found at ancient Bethel, gives archaeological evidence, not only of Ophir having an

179. *The Temple Site*

180. *Sealed Entrance to Quarry*

181. *Quarry beneath Jerusalem*

182. *Wailing Wall*

183. *Hitching Posts*

184. *Gezer Calendar*

185. *Solomon's Pool*

186. *Conduits from Solomon's Pools*

187. *Vessels of Gold*

188. *Ophir Ostracon*

abundance of gold, but that extensive trade was carried on between Israel and Sheba. This supports the queen of Sheba's visit to see Solomon (I Kings 10: 1-13). (See "Solomon's Copper Mines," p. 51.) *No. 189* shows the "star" of Solomon on the ruins of a synagogue at Capernaum.

The United Kingdom of Israel lasted 120 years. Each king reigned 40 years: Saul (Acts 13:21), David (II Sam. 5: 4), and Solomon (I Kings 11:42). Just before Solomon's death, the prophet Ahijah predicted that God would rend the kingdom out of Solomon's hand because he forsook the Lord, worshiped other gods, and did not walk in the ways of the Lord and keep His statutes (I Kings 11:29-33).

189. Solomon's Star

THE DIVIDED KINGDOM

After the death of Solomon, the people went to Shechem to make Rehoboam their king. They sent for Jeroboam, who had fled to Egypt because Solomon threatened to take his life (I Kings 11: 40). Jeroboam, with the people, requested relief from the heavy taxes and burdens laid upon them by king Solomon. After three days counsel with Israel's leaders, Rehoboam rejected their plea. The people rebelled, stoned the tax collector, renounced the family of David and set Jeroboam over them as king. Only two tribes, Judah and Benjamin, remained loyal to Rehoboam, and made Jerusalem their capital. Jeroboam and the leaders of the other ten tribes settled in Shechem (Samaria later became the capital). Rehoboam assembled 180,000 fighting men to force the followers of Jeroboam to submit to him, but was forbidden of the Lord through the prophet Shemaiah, saying, "this [division] is of me" (I Kings 12:1-24a). This division brought Judah under the watchful eye of the Lord, so that, in spite of sin, corrup-

tion, idolatry, and being scattered without a king for years, Judah's people would not be "lost" — the Word of God would be fulfilled in the coming of Israel's Messiah and the world's Saviour. "The sceptre shall not depart from Judah, nor a lawgiver from beneath his feet, until Shiloh [Christ] come" (Gen. 49:10).

THE (NORTHERN) KINGDOM OF ISRAEL

The approximate date of the Kingdom of Israel is from Jeroboam, 931 B.C. to Hoshea, 722 B.C. Not a single king of this Kingdom did good in God's sight — all were evil. Graven images were substituted for God, and high places were built for worship of these idols. Farmers were induced to take up practices of the fertility cult to insure crops. Amos warned Israel to seek God and live, but not at Bethel, where Jeroboam had set up "golden calves" (Amos 5:4; I Kings 12:28, 29). He also condemned Israel for "sacred prostitution," which resulted from this type of worship (2:8). Hosea accused them of many sins associated with Baal worship, such as "lewdness in the sight of her lovers" (2:10-13); whoredom, adultery, making sacrifices with harlots (4:14; 5:4); sacrificing to and kissing the golden calves (13:2); and for not crying to God, the most High (7: 18:45). (See "Baal Worship," p. 119.) land with Baalism. Elijah walked into Ahab's palace (No. 194) and told him that a famine would befall the land. After judgment came because Israel had halted between God and Baal, God's name was vindicated (I Kings 16:28— 18:45). (See "Baal Worship," p. 119.)

God began to "stir" the hearts of heathen peoples to bring His people to their knees. Prophets were raised to warn Israel, but they would not heed their voices. Many pagan kings fought against them — Mesha of Moab, Shalmaneser III, V, Tiglath-peleser (or Pul), and Sargon of Assyria. *No. 190* is the old Assyrian Pass at Dog River, north of Beirut, Lebanon, over which the Assyrian armies crossed the Lebanon mountains to war against Samaria. Tribute was paid to the invaders to keep Israel from being taken captive (II Kings 15: 19). Little by little some Jews were taken captive (I Chron. 5:25, 26; II Kings 15:27-29). Finally, King Sargon captured Samaria, and the remaining subjects of the Northern Kingdom were

190. Old Assyrian Pass

taken captive (II Kings 17:1-24; 18:11, 12). Under the seige of Samaria by Shalmaneser and after its capture by Sargon, Assyrians were brought into the cities of Samaria to re-settle the land. An Israelite priest was returned from captivity to teach these people about the true and living God (II Kings 17:26-28). These "foreigners" in Israel's territory later became known as the "Samaritans" (No. 265).

The reader must constantly be reminded that critics of the Bible are something like Satan — they never sleep (Matt. 13:24, 25). Until certain discoveries by the archaeologists, they claimed that the names of many "foreign" kings in the Bible were fictitious because none of their names were recorded in secular history, thus making the portions of Scripture which contain these names, and the historical events to which they relate, false or fable. It was not until God "made stones cry out" that many of these names were found to be attached to "real, live human beings."

After the capital of the Northern Kingdom was moved to Samaria, King Omri made Mesha, king of Moab, pay tribute to him. Part of the tribute was sheep's wool. Mesha was supposed to be a fictitious character, and Moab was too barren (the critics said) to graze sheep. In 1868, there was discovered in the city of Diban (in Moab) what is called the "Moabite Stone" *(No. 191)*. This inscribed object is four feet high, two feet wide, and fourteen inches thick. A part of the records says, *"I, Mesha, king of Moab, made this monument to Chemosh* [god of Moab] *to commemorate my deliverance from Israel. . . . Omri, king of Israel oppressed Moab and his son* [Ahab] *after him. I warred against their cities, devoted the spoil to Chemosh, and in Beth-Diblathaim sheep raisers I placed."* This "dead stone" confirms II

191. *The Moabite Stone*

Kings 3:4, 5. Not only does it prove that Mesha was not a fictitious character, it lends support that sections of Moab were sufficiently fertile for raising sheep to produce wool as tribute to King Omri.

Samaria was located on top of a mountain, completely encircled by a valley. Beyond lay mountain ranges which surrounded the valley. This strategic location on a hilltop (No. 76) enabled a lone watchman to see the approach of an enemy from any point. Ezekiel used this to illustrate our need to stand as a watchman against the enemy of our souls (3: 17-21). Because of this natural fortification which surrounded Samaria, Israel had made these mountains her trust, and God was forgotten. This prompted Amos to thunder, "Woe unto them that are at ease in Zion and trust in the mountains of Samaria" (6:1). Looking beyond the ruins of Herod's summer palace (*No. 192*), which was built over the ruins of Ahab's palace, one can see the valley

192. *Ruins at Samaria*

which lies between the city and the mountains beyond. Amos sought to warn of the evils of prosperity, and of security in military might. He condemned them for putting "far away the evil day, causing violence to come near, lying upon beds of ivory, inventing music, drinking wine, and anointing themselves with costly perfumes and ointments." He then predicted that they "shall go captive" (6: 1-8). King Ahab had built an ivory palace at Samaria (I Kings 22:39), and thousands of ivory carvings, some of which are seen (*No. 193*), give evidence that the Israelites had indeed given in to the fad of their day, thus robbing God of His tithes (Amos 6:4; 4:4). *No. 194* shows the ruins of and entrance to Ahab's ivory palace. It was up these steps, no doubt, that old Elijah walked as he marched himself into the presence of King Ahab and announced the famine to come because of sin in the land (I Kings 17:1).

193. Samaritan Ivory

194. Entrance to Ahab's Palace

Archaeological discoveries often give additional information on Old Testament activities which are not recorded in the Bible. The Black Obelisk (*No. 195*) of Shalmaneser III, king of Assyria, was found in the ruins of his palace at Calah (Nimrud). It shows officials of five different nations paying tribute to Shalnameser, one of whom is Israel's King Jehu (II Kings 9—10; *No. 196*). The record above mentions *"Tribute of Jehu, son* [or descendant] *of Omri, gold, silver, golden goblets and pitchers, golden vases and vessels, scepters from the hand of the king, javelins I received from him."* The obelisk, six and one-half feet tall, bears the only contemporary likeness that has ever been found of any Israelite king.

Further archaeological confirmation of Shalmaneser III is seen at the top of the

195. The Black Obelisk

196. King Jehu

197. Shalmaneser and Inscription

Assyrian Pass (No. 190). He is shown (*No. 197*) on the left, with an inscription of his exploits, having aligned his armies with an Egyptian army against Israel at Samaria (right). One of Shalmaneser's inscriptions refers to himself as *"the legitimate King, King of the Universe, the King without rival, the 'Great Dragon,' the only power within the four rims of the whole world . . . , who smashed all his foes like pots."*

Before the rise of Tiglath-peleser III, possibly in the reign of Ashur-dan III (772-755 B.C.), the prophet Jonah was commanded to go to Assyria's principal city, Nineveh, and preach repentance. This was during the reign of Jeroboam II of Israel (II Kings 14:23-25). There was a time when some critics seriously doubted the size of Nineveh's population as recorded in the book of Jonah (4:11). They felt that no city in that day had a population of 120,000. Excavations at Nimrud, some twenty miles from Nineveh, produced a large monument of King Ashurnasipal II, whose Assyrian armies first began to make assault on Israel. Among other things he listed on this inscription (*No. 198*) was the menu for a banquet at the dedication of his palace when 70,000 were fed. Those in atten-

198. Ashurnasipal's Monument

dance were the "chief" people of Nimrud, which implies that many, many more inhabited the city. It confirms that cities in that day, just as the Bible states, were heavily populated.

199. Tiglath-pileser

God stirred the spirit of Tiglath-pileser (*No. 199*) to come against His people (II Kings 15:29; I Chron. 5:26). In his royal annals Tiglath makes a number of references to Old Testament characters, naming Azariah of Judah and Menahem of Samaria who paid him tribute. He said he replaced Pekah with Hoshea on the throne of Israel during his campaign in Palestine in 734-732 B.C. An interesting sidelight as to how archaeology sometimes sheds light on Biblical customs is the third man in the chariot (left, No. 199) — the "lord [servant] on whose hand the king leaned" (II Kings 7:2). This servant's responsibility as a "strap hanger" was to protect the king from falling backward as he rode in his chariot. (It might appear in I Chron. 5:26 that "Pul" and "Tiglath-pileser" of Assyria were two different kings. The expression "and the spirit of Tiglath . . ." should be "even the spirit . . . and *he*" — singular — carried them away. Many scholars believe the two mentioned are one and the same.)

According to II Kings Shalmaneser V started the final seige of Samaria. According to the records of the Assyrians it would seem that Shalmaneser died and Sargon actually captured the city. The only reference of Sargon's name for centuries was the Bible, and that in parenthesis (Isa. 20:1). This was one of the Bible's biggest errors, so said the critics, because no other record contained his name. Isaiah stated that Sargon sent Tartan and captured Ashdod. However, it is interesting to note that the Bible does not say that Shalmaneser actually captured Samaria. The Record states that "they" took it (II Kings 18:9) and this could very well mean the one who started the seige and the one who finished its capture.

Did Sargon actually exist? Archaeological discoveries answer in the affirmative. His palace at Khorsabad was unearthed, along with statues (*No. 200*) and records.

200. Sargon

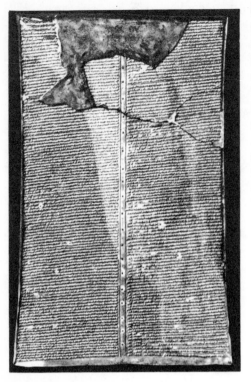

201. *Sargon's Record*

One record is confirmation of Isaiah's statement: *"Ashdod's king, Azuri, plotted to avoid paying me tribute. In anger I marched against Ashdod with my captain, conquering."* Just within recent years the "Ashdod Excavation Project" found an inscription of Sargon's at Ashdod which actually confirmed his conquest there. Another inscription found at Khorsabad states that Shalmaneser died while fighting at Samaria, and that he, Sargon, succeeded him. He even mentioned the number of Israelites he deported — 27,-290 (*No. 201*). He then rebuilt Samaria, settled Assyrians in the cities and placed an officer over them as governor.

His palace occupied some twenty-five acres, and its walls were from nine to about sixteen feet in thickness. Large stone "winged-bulls" (*No. 202*), stood at its entrance. Inscribed bricks had identity as to whose palace it was — *"I, Sargon, have erected this house for mine own glory"* (*No. 203*). In the palace

202. *"Winged Bulls"*

203. *Sargon's Brick*

204. *Counting Hands*

courtyard were three temples, a towering ziggurat, luxurious harems and spacious domestic quarters.

Over and above the glory and might of the Assyrian kings, a brutality possessed them which has seldom been duplicated in the course of history. Victors in battle, accountable for those they slew, would cut off the hands of the slain and give them to scribes to count (*No. 204*). The monument below (*No. 205*) shows the triumphal return of armies with heads, bound prisoners, women and children. Ashurbanipal, probably the "great and noble Asnapper" of Ezra 4:10 (see also pp. 67, 73), boasted that he flayed

205. *Heads of Prisoners*

206. Blinding Prisoners

all those who rebelled against him, taking their skins and covering the pillars of his temple. One king boasted that he burned three thousand captives with fire. Another king recorded: *"Monuments I erected I used human bodies after I severed their heads and limbs."* Another brutal punishment, mainly for treason, was putting out the eyes of traitors (*No. 206*). Hooks and rings were placed in jaws and tongues and feet were bound, forcing prisoners to take short steps. If some could not keep "pace" while being marched, the conqueror would give a yank of the leash and "from their hostile mouths tongues were torn out by their roots." Torture such as this also helped to break their resistance. Nebuchadnezzar, king of Babylon, "put out the eyes of Zedekiah" (II Kings 25:7), using the same method of Sargon (No. 206). King Manassah was taken with hooks (II Chron. 33:11 R.V.). These cruel and brutal acts were done in accordance with the martial laws of Assyria and Babylon. It is said of Sargon that his acts of brutality were for "propaganda purposes," and brought Assyria to a pinnacle of savage grandeur. Is it any wonder that

God's prophets warned Israel to repent and return to the Lord, lest they be defeated and taken into captivity?

THE (SOUTHERN) KINGDOM OF JUDAH

The approximate date of this kingdom is from Rehoboam to Zedekiah (931-587 B.C.). Of her twenty kings it is recorded of only eight that "they did that which was right in the Lord's sight" (Asa — I Kings 15:11; Jehosaphat — I Kings 22: 43; Joash — II Kings 12:2; Amaziah — II Kings 14:3; Uzziah — II Kings 15:3; Jotham — II Kings 15:34; Hezekiah — II Kings 18:3; Josiah — II Kings 22:2).

No sooner had this kingdom been established than king Rehoboam built "high places, images and groves on every high hill. . . . And there were also sodomites in the land: and they did according to all the abominations" of those in Canaan (I Kings 14:21-24). Because Rehoboam "forsook the law of the Lord, and all Israel with him . . . Shishak, king of Egypt, came up against Jerusalem, because Israel had transgressed against the Lord . . . and took away the treasures of the house of the Lord and the king's house; he took all: he carried away the shields of gold which Solomon had made" (II Chron. 12). King Shishak inscribed his own record of this invasion of Judah. He dedicated the spoils to his god Amon, pictured in the center, and listed the conquered cities of Judah on the figures below and back of Amon. These figures also represented captured Israelites (*No. 207*). This is but another instance where a record of secular history confirms a portion of the Word of God. In 1939 Shishak's mummy was found in a silver coffin, which had been placed inside a gold case. Who knows but what this case might have been made from the gold of Solomon's shields.

Archaeologists recently discovered a fort believed to have been built by King Uzziah, who reigned in the days of Elijah. A secret passage in the wall has illuminated several accounts in Scripture. Until this discovery, one could only guess about the building tricks involved when Old Testament characters by-passed the gates of fortified cities to sneak in or out. This fort had casement walls, actually two walls with passage separating them by a few yards. The outer wall was built with oblong stones about three feet long and a foot square. One of these stones, closely fitted to the others, could be slipped out, revealing steps which led into the city. A stranger on the outside would

207. Shishak's Invasion Record of Judah

208. *Seal of Shema*

not know which one of the many wall-stones concealed the secret entrance. The book of Judges tells of spies from Israel's army at Bethel seeking the secret passage. They asked a man outside the city wall, "Pray, show us the way into the city, and we will deal kindly with thee" (Judg. 1:24). The man did and the army sneaked into Bethel. A secret passage saved the people of Jerusalem when Nebuchadnezzar broke into the city: "The king with all his men of war fled by night by the way of the gate between two walls . . ." (II Kings 25:4).

A number of seals have been found in excavations. The word "seal" is a term to describe both the device for making an impression, and the impression itself. The use of a seal to authenticate a document is an ancient Biblical custom. Its impression corresponds to the Western habit of writing one's signature. When Ahab sought to purchase Naboth's vineyard and was refused, his wife, Jezebel, deceivingly wrote letters to the elders of Naboth's city, giving instructions for him to be slain. She wrote these letters in Ahab's name, sealing them with his seal, thus making her murder plans "official" (I Kings 21:1-16). One discovered seal is that of "Shema, servant of Jeroboam" (*No. 208*). The word "servant" means minister, equivalent of the office of

"Prime Minister" or "Secretary of State." The seal of King Jotham (*No. 209*) was discovered when the Red Sea-port city of Ezion-geber was excavated. This is the only seal yet discovered of Israel's kings. Each seal, Shema's and Jotham's, has the figure of the lion, the symbol of Judah. Christ is referred to as the "Lion of the tribe of Judah" (Rev. 5:5).

Hezekiah became the thirteenth king of Judah. He did that which was right in the sight of the Lord, removing the high places, breaking images and cutting down groves (II Kings 18:1-7). Second Kings 20:20 speaks of his acts, and how he built a conduit to bring water into the city of Jerusalem. This verse had been ridiculed by critics, who not only said the writer had sought to enhance Hezekiah's position with the remark of his mighty acts, but that it was utterly false because no one knew of the existence of any such conduit.

Jerusalem depended upon the Spring of Gihon (*No. 210*) and other wells located

209. *King Jotham's Signet Ring and Impression*

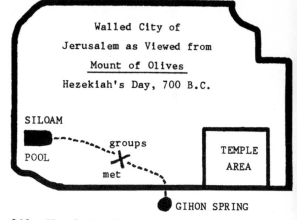

211. Pool of Siloam

210. Spring of Gihon

outside the city wall for their water supply. In times of seige, city wall gates had to be closed, and many times citizens surrendered due to a lack of food and water. Long before David's day the Jebusites hacked a tunnel through solid rock from Gihon and sank a forty-foot shaft from above to connect the city with the water channel. Scripture hints that David's general Joab captured Jerusalem through this shaft (II Sam. 5:8).

Three hundred years after the Jebusites brought water into the city from the Spring, Hezekiah, in realizing the need for water in times of war, had his men dig a conduit from the Spring to the Pool of Siloam, which he built inside the city wall (*No. 211*). The diagram (*No. 212*) shows how Hezekiah accomplished this bit of engineering. Giving his men instructions, he put a group of pickmen where the Jebusites dug (No. 210), and

Walled City of
Jerusalem as Viewed from
Mount of Olives
Hezekiah's Day, 700 B.C.

SILOAM

POOL

groups

met

TEMPLE
AREA

GIHON SPRING

212. Hezekiah's Conduit Plans

another group at the Pool of Siloam. At a given signal, both groups started digging, tunneling their way beneath Jerusalem. When the two groups were about four and a half feet apart, they called to each other, and soon met face to face at the point indicated (*No. 213*).

How do we know that this is Hezekiah's conduit, and that he built it? In 1890, a truant boy wading inside the conduit at the Pool of Siloam found an

213. *Where Pickmen Met*

214. *Hezekiah's Inscription*

inscription which gave evidence to this very fact. The inscription (*No. 214*) is one of the oldest in the Hebrew language, and reads as follows: *"This is the history of the excavation. While workmen still lifting up their axe* [pick], *each toward his neighbors, and while three cubits remain* [to cut through], *each heard voices calling one to another. On the day the workmen struck, axe against axe, to meet his neighbors, waters flowed from the* [Gihon] *Spring to* [Siloam] *Pool a thousand and two hundred cubits; and a hundred cubits the height over the heads of the workmen."* Entering at the Spring of Gihon (No. 210), one notices pick marks in the direction he is moving. The author is pointing to the place where the two groups of pickmen met (No. 213), and from here on through the conduit to the Pool of Siloam the pick marks were in the opposite direction. The cubit of Hezekiah's time was eighteen inches, making the conduit 1,800 feet long, and 150 feet below the city. Its average width was about 27 inches, and a little over six feet high. The conduit, cut through solid rock, *is* testimony that Hezekiah did exactly what the Bible says he did.

King Sennacherib of Assyria beseiged forty-six cities in the land of Judah, one of which was Lachish. When archaeologists discovered Sennacherib's palace, a monument (*No. 215*) and a record showed an officer of Lachish bringing tribute to the Assyrian king. The record stated that Hezekiah paid him thirty tal-

215. *Sennacherib's Monument*

ents of gold and eight hundred silver talents. This record contradicted the Biblical account of Hezekiah's tribute to Sennacherib as found in II Kings 18: 13-16. Of course, the Bible critic had a field day — until another record was unearthed which listed measurements and weights. This record stated it took eight hundred Assyrian talents of silver to equal three hundred Hebrew silver talents. Once again archaeology has confirmed another passage of Scripture.

After the fall of Lachish, Sennacherib advanced toward Jerusalem and demanded Hezekiah surrender to his armies. God intervened because of King Hezekiah's prayer and delivered His people (II Kings 18, 19). In Sennacherib's own record of his seige of Jerusalem (*No. 216*) he said, *"himself* [Hezekiah] *like a caged bird I shut up in Jerusalem and earthworks I threw against him; the one coming out of the city* [Hezekiah's messenger], *I turned back to his own misery."* No actual claim is made of capturing Jerusalem itself, implying that he withdrew without successfully defeating King Hezekiah. This certainly lends support to the Bible claim that God did deliver the royal city of Jerusalem. While Sennacherib was careful to give details of his battles and victories, such as his seige of Jerusalem, and receiving tribute after defeating Lachish, he was even more careful to "leave out" anything that might spell "defeat." (The battle of the Assyrians against Jerusalem was carved on a monument found in the ruins of Sennacherib's palace, No. 20.)

That King Hezekiah was mighty in prayer is borne out in the miracle that God performed in prolonging his life fifteen years (II Kings 20:1-21). When he died, it is said of him that he "slept with his fathers." The expression, "slept with his fathers," was used of many of the kings of Judah, referring to their final

216. Sennacherib's Prism

217. Tombs of
the Kings

resting place. There are thirty-nine ancient rock-hewn vaults in the city of Jerusalem today which convey to us what the
"Tombs of the Kings of Judah" might
have looked like (No. 217). The entrance was sealed with a rolling stone
(No. 218 — end view).

Manasseh ascended the throne after
his father (Hezekiah) died, and became
the worst of all the kings of both Kingdoms (II Kings 21:1-16). It was during
his reign that the "captains of the host of
the king of Assyria" put him in chains
and carried him to Babylon (II Chron.
33:9-11). Second Kings 19:37 would im-
ply that Sennacherib's son, Esarhaddon,
was the Assyrian king who had Manasseh captured. Esarhaddon's own record
makes certain he was the king. He mentions Manasseh as follows: *"I summoned
the kings of the Hittite-land* [Syria] *and*
[those] *across the sea . . . Ba'lu, King
of Tyre, Manasseh, King of Judah, Kaush-
gabri, King of Edom. . . . I gave them
orders."* Critics of the Bible questioned
Babylon as the site of Manasseh's cap-

218. Rolling Stone

219. Esarhaddon

tivity because Sennacherib had utterly destroyed this city during his reign. Archaeological records show that Esarhaddon rebuilt Babylon, making it a magnificent city (probably because his wife and mother were from Babylon). *No. 219* shows a monument of Esarhaddon and an inscription of his at Dog River, which is adjacent to Shalmaneser's (No. 197). Here he tells that his dominion extended all the way through Palestine down to Egypt. Ezra (4:1, 2) mentions this king as one who helped to colonize Samaria. (The Northern Kingdom fell in 722 B.C. Esarhaddon reigned from *ca.* 681-668 B.C. Manasseh ruled from *ca.* 687-642 B.C.)

BABYLONIAN CAPTIVITY

When Jehoiakim became king over Judah, Nebuchadnezzar, king of Babylon came to Jerusalem and made him his servant. In servitude for three years, Jehoiakim rebelled, and the Lord sent judgment on him for the innocent blood he shed. Nebuchadnezzar bound him in fetters (chains) and carried him and the vessels of the house of the Lord to Babylon (II Kings 24:1-5; II Chron. 36:5-7). Listed in the first deportation to Babylon was Daniel (Dan. 1:1-6).

The second deportation took place under the reign of Jehoiachin, when Nebuchadnezzar came back and took Jehoiachin and all his mighty men of valor to Babylon. He destroyed the vessels of the Temple (which had replaced the ones previously taken by Nebuchadnezzar), and left the poorest of the people to remain in the land (II Kings 24:8-16; II Chron. 36:9, 10). Ezekiel was included in this second group (Ezek. 1:1, 2). Other cities were attacked by Nebuchadnezzar — Lachish, which had been rebuilt, and Azekiah. The seal of Gedaliah, ruler of those remaining in the land, has been found (*No. 220*). See II Kings 25: 27-30 and "Lachish Letters," p. 46.

The third and final deportation took place under King Zedekiah. This time, Nebuchadnezzar put a blockade around Jerusalem, causing famine. When the people tried to flee he captured them, set fire to the whole city, and broke down its wall. He showed no compassion — all were taken captive except the poorest of

220. Seal of Gedaliah

221. *Captives Bound for Babylon*

the poor, who were left to till the soil (II Kings 25:1-21; II Chron. 36:11-21). The final overthrow of the Southern Kingdom of Judah is recorded in these words: "So Judah was carried away out of their land" (II Kings 25:21), and remained in captivity for seventy years until the Medes and Persians defeated the Babylonians (II Chron. 36:20-23).

Judah's captivity was foretold by Moses (Deut. 28:36, 47-52). Their captivity was again foretold 150 years before it happened (Isa. 6:11, 12), and Babylon was predicted as the place of captivity (Micah 4:9, 10). Jeremiah informs us that these predictions were fulfilled when Nebuchadnezzar made his three attacks on Jerusalem (52:27-30). How marvelously accurate is the Word of God, confirmed by history itself and by the archaeologist's evidence.

Scripture gives us at least four reasons why God permitted Judah to be taken into captivity for seventy years:

1. Failure to keep the Sabbatical year (Lev. 25:1-7). The result of this failure

was captivity (Lev. 26:27, 33-35). Jeremiah said captivity was to "fulfill the Word of the Lord" (II Chron. 36:20, 21). It would seem that from the time of the dedication of the Temple until Israel's captivity, about 490 years, the Sabbatical year had not been kept. By dividing 7 into 490, we get 70, the number of years Israel spent in Babylon "until the land enjoyed her sabbaths."

2. Ungratefulness. God had been faithful to His Word in bringing Israel

222. *Babylonian Chronicle*

into the land, but Israel had ignored His claims upon her. Baalism was embraced, and marriage to unbelievers became common (Judg. 3:5-7). Sex was idolized, and groves, the symbol of sex and fertility, were erected *in* the house of God (I Kings 14:24; II Kings 21:7; 23:6, 7). Incense was burned to the brazen serpent that Moses made, and their children were offered to Baal and demons as human sacrifices (II Kings 18:4; Jer. 19:4, 5; Ps. 106:37, 38). Manasseh "seduced them to do *more* evil than did the nations whom the Lord destroyed before the children of Israel" (II Kings 21:1-9).

Israel was the most ungrateful, the most unstable, and perhaps the most sinful nation that ever existed. (I say this in view of her calling above all other nations, and the light which God had given to her of Himself — II Chron. 36:14-16.) Isaiah tells us that God labeled them "rulers of Sodom — people of Gomorrah," and that if it had not been for a faithful remnant, God would have destroyed them (Isa. 1:9, 10). Of course, judgment came to Israel — "The wrath of the Lord arose against his people till there was no remedy" — no remedy for their being taken into captivity. What a sad testimony for a nation which received so much from God's hand, but failed to walk in the light of His Word.

3. Strange gods, who automatically became a part of ungratefulness (Deut. 28:36; 31:16, 20; Judg. 10:6; I Kings 11:33).

4. Touching God's anointed. God had warned, "Touch not mine anointed, and do my prophets no harm" (I Chron. 16:22). But Israel did, and God's longsuffering and patience came to an end (II Chron. 36:15, 16).

No. 221 shows captured Israelites being taken to Babylon. *No. 222* is "The Babylonian Chronicle" for 605-594 B.C., which describes the battle of Charchemish (II Chron. 35:20), mentions the coronation of Nebuchadnezzar, the removal of Jehoiachin and others to Babylonian exile, and lists their rations (II Kings 25:27-30). It states that Zedekiah was enthroned in King Jehoiachin's place, giving March 16, 597 B.C., the date for Jerusalem's capture in the first seige. Ten years later, 587 B.C., Jerusalem was destroyed.

No. 223 is an air-view of Babylon's mound. Babylon, once a world center of power and glory, is now a pile of dust

223. *Air View of Babylon*

154

224. *Nebuchadnezzar*

225. *Ruins of Babylon*

and broken-down walls. *No. 224* is a cameo bearing the likeness of Nebuchadnezzar. The inscription which surrounds his portrait says, *"Nebuchadnezzar King of Babylon."* He was king from 604-561 B.C. This carving was taken from a black stone which was dedicated to his god Merodack. (Jeremiah predicted both Babylon's and Merodach's downfall; 50: 1-3.) *No. 225* shows the ruins of Babylon as seen today. *No. 226* shows the probable ruins of Nebuchadnezzar's "Hanging Gardens." *No. 227* is a brick from Nebuchadnezzar's palace, bearing his

226. *Hanging Gardens*

227. *Nebuchadnezzar's Brick*

228. *Processional Street*

inscription — *"I Nebuchandezzar have built this palace to mine own praise."* *No. 228* shows "Processional Street," which led into Babylon through the Ishtar gate. The captured Israelites marched over this same pavement as they entered Babylon. *No. 229* is the goddess Ishtar, the goddess of War, who was revered in Babylon. She supposedly gave the Babylonians their victories.

The Ishtar Gate (*No. 230*), which was dedicated to the goddess Ishtar, is one of the most impressive monuments discovered in the ancient East. The gateway, flanked by twin towers and ornamented with pinnacles, was covered with colored enamelled bricks. Dragons and bulls, which symbolized the gods Marduk and Adad, were bright yellow and brown, surrounded by blue tiles. The gate (No.

230) was reconstructed out of material excavated at Babylon, and is forty-seven feet high.

The artist's conception of ancient Babylon (*No. 231*), shows "Procession Street" going through the Ishtar Gate. Inside, the "Sacred Way" led past Nebuchadnezzar's palace to the seven-storied ziggurat, crowned by the temple of Marduk ("Hanging Gardens" are back of palace on right). Some archaeologists are of the opinion that this ziggurat was built on the foundation ruins of the "Tower of Babel" mentioned in Genesis 11:1-9. It was called the "House of the Foundation of Heaven and Earth."

The "Hanging Gardens," built by Nebuchadnezzar for one of his wives, was regarded as one of the "Seven Wonders" of the ancient world. The palace dining room was a mile long and one-third of a mile wide. Huge stone elephants twenty

229. *Goddess Ishtar*

230. *Ishtar Gate*

231. *Babylon Restored*

feet high were placed about the room. On each stood a tall bronze statue of a slave. With one foot on the head of the elephant and the other on its hip, the slave, with outstretched hands, held a chain which linked him to the next figure. The chains supported the "Hanging Gardens."

The ancient historian, Herodotus, said Babylon's wall was 60 miles in length, 15 miles on each side, 300 feet high and 80 feet thick. Over 250 pillars (monuments) had been erected to her war lords, from 50 to 250 feet high. In the city's center were 150 pillars, 88 feet high and 19 feet in diameter, supporting a chapel of solid marble. It contained an image of the god "Bel," 40 feet high and overlaid with solid gold. Young girls sold their virtue to the highest bidder at this shrine. It is said at one time 10,000 girls stood with broken hearts because their virtue had not been sold for sacred sex acts. "The glory of kingdoms, the beauty of the Chaldees' excellency" was Isaiah's description of Babylon (13:19). Nebuchadnezzar boasted to Daniel, saying, "This great Babylon" (4:30).

When Nebuchadnezzar dreamed dreams and commanded his magicians and astrologers to give their interpretations, they failed. Daniel correctly interpreted them. Because of this, Daniel was promoted (chap. 2). An interesting discovery in Babylon revealed the ruins of a college, a library and curricula for native princes, to be trained especially for interpretations of dreams and visions. On one record were given two regulations: 1. Impiety to any gods — cast alive into a fiery furnace; 2. Untoward act relative to a king — cast alive into the den of lions.

Nebuchadnezzar's pride is seen in his "image of gold" and the command for all people to worship it. It was ninety feet high and nine feet wide. Discovered records show that Nebuchadnezzar's custom, not only in Babylon but also at Ur of the Chaldees, was to make public the worshiping of images. The three Hebrew children refused to bow to this image and were punished by being thrown alive into a fiery furnace. Deliverance by God of these three boys resulted in Nebuchadnezzar's recognition of Israel's God (Dan. 3:1—4:3). Excavators at Babylon found this very furnace, with an inscription: "This is the place of burning where men who blasphemed the gods of Chaldea die by fire."

In spite of Babylon's might and beauty, God predicted the Medes would overthrow their kingdom as He had overthrown Sodom and Gomorrah. "It shall never be inhabited, it shall not be dwelt in from generation to generation, neither shall the Arabian pitch tent there nor the shepherd make his fold there. But wild beasts shall lie there and their houses shall be full of doleful creatures. It shall becomes heaps . . . , an astonishment, and an hissing, without an inhabitant" (Isa. 13:17-22; Jer. 51:37-43). The excavated ruins of Babylon confirm God's Word, both to its beauty and its destruction and desolation. Present day mounds are found East of the river (No. 223).

The dining room beneath the "Hanging Gardens" was, no doubt, the one in which Belshazzar held his great feast and saw the "handwriting on the wall" (Dan. 5). It was this king who was killed when the Medes and Persians took Babylon, and the Bible mentions him as the *last* king of this kingdom. A clay tablet revealed that *Nabonidus* was the last king of Babylon, and that he was allowed by the Persians to live out his life in retirement. Naturally, the critics were quick to condemn the Scriptures. But a research among hundreds of clay tablets which told about the reign of Nabonidus showed that he had a son by the name of Belshazzar, who was "regent" in his stead.

This was common practice in those days — to appoint a son to reign in his father's place. While Nabonidus was in one of his palaces remote from Babylon, Belshazzar was king when Babylon fell. We can understand better Belshazzar's saying that if Daniel could interpret his dream he would "be the *third* ruler in the kingdom" (Dan. 5:16). He couldn't have been made the first — that was Nabonidus' position. Belshazzar was second, so Daniel was offered the position next to the *reigning* monarch. This shows that Daniel's historical record *is* accurate. Once again archaeology and the Bible are in agreement.

After the Medes and Persians captured Babylon, Daniel was elevated to a high position over the whole kingdom. Because of his faithfulness to the God of Israel, others in authority sought to bring him in disrepute with King Darius by the issuing of a decree that no one should ask of any god a petition, save the king only. Daniel prayed to his God in spite of the decree, and King Darius (*No. 232*) was forced to throw Daniel in the lion's den (*No. 233; Dan. 6:4-17*).

Discovered at this site was an inscription: *"The place of execution where men who angered the king die, torn by wild beasts."* King Darius had his image and exploits sculptured at Behistun Rock in ancient Persia, or modern Iraq (No. 97), telling of leading his troops into Babylon, and shows him giving thanks to his winged-god "Ahuramazda" for victories (*No. 234*). Part of the inscription says: *"I am Darius. By the grace of Ahuramazda I am ruler of 23 lands including Babylonia, Sparda [Sardis?] Arabia, Egypt. . . . I put down rebellions of Gaumata and eight other lands in nineteen battles. . . ."* To give an idea how kings of old "enhanced" their positions, the monument of Darius at Behistun Rock is a good example. He is exactly six feet tall, his lords back of him are exactly five feet tall, and his captive enemies in front of him are exactly four feet tall. A defeated king lies beneath his foot with upraised arms, begging for mercy.

RETURN FROM CAPTIVITY

When kings Darius and Cyrus were established in Babylon, the seventy year

232. King Darius

233. *Lion's Den*

captivity of Judah came to an end (Dan. 10:1, 2). Israel was now subject to their rule. Cyrus was prophetically named by Isaiah more than a century before his birth that he would be the king who would give Judah permission to return to their homeland and rebuild their Temple and Jerusalem (Isa. 44:28—45:1). Cyrus issued a decree (Ezra 1:1-4), thus fulfilling God's Word. The decree lists his genealogy and tells how the great city of Babylon surrendered to him without resistance (which confirms Daniel's account). King Darius, who acted as vice-regent for Cyrus, took Babylon in the name of Cyrus, "King of the host, the great King." Cyrus later entered Babylon, presented himself in the role of the "liberator of the people," and permitted the liberated captives to return to their original cities. His decree, quite naturally, included all of the Hebrew people. This decree was discovered and is now in the British Museum, London (*No. 235*). His palace and his tomb (*No. 236*) have also been found.

The city of Persepolis was built by King Darius, and was the principal cap-

234. *God Ahuramazda*

235. *Decree of Cyrus*

236. *Tomb of Cyrus*

237. *Ceremonial Stairway*

ital of Persia. Ruins of the Ceremonial Staircase (*No. 237*) lead to the huge audience hall in the city, located near the palaces of Darius and his son, Xerxes. The reliefs on the stairway show envoys of twenty-three subject nations bringing New Year's gifts to Persia's kings. The reception hall originally had one hundred columns but only a few are standing today.

Nehemiah, like Daniel, was given a place of trust and confidence by King Artaxerxes, grandson of King Darius. He was the king's "cupbearer" (*No. 238*; Neh. 1:11; 2:1). The gold cup (*No. 239*) shows Persian craftsmanship of 510 B.C., a type used by "cupbearers" of Nehemiah's day.

Ezra, the scribe, had a decree made in his behalf by Artaxerxes (Ezra 7:11-29). One of his decrees (*No. 240*) gives us an idea what Ezra's looked like. The "laws" of the "Medes and Persians" were never changed. That is why King Darius

was forced to cast Daniel in the lion's den (Dan. 6:1-7). When God prophesied that Cyrus would permit Israel to return after their captivity, He knew that the decree could not be altered, thereby assuring Israel of her return to the Promised Land and Jerusalem.

Old Testament history ends with the records found in Ezra, Nehemiah, and

238. *King's Cupbearer*

239. *Persian Gold Cup*

Esther. Ezra and Nehemiah relate the account of those who returned home and rebuilt the city of Jerusalem and the Temple. Esther gives the account of those who chose to remain in Babylonia. Remains of Queen Esther's palace, located at Shushan (Susa, Persia), have been located. On the basis of what was discovered (wall foundations, rooms, records, etc.) a model of the palace has been made. The throne room had thirty-six fluted columns and one can locate the "king's gate" where Mordecai worried Haman; the "inner court of the king's house" where Esther appeared without being bidden by the king; the "outward court of the king's house," where Haman came to ask that Mordecai be hanged; and the "palace garden," where the king went to cool off his anger against Haman (Esther 5:1; 6:4; 7:7). The discovery of this palace by archaeologists shows that the setting of the book of Esther truly depicts Persian customs and life.

Israel's history, from Egypt to Captivity, even to the coming of Christ, was a series of "ups and downs." In the wilderness she murmured and complained. In the land she broke God's covenant and served other gods. In captivity she lost her song (Ps. 137:1-4). Even when she returned to the land and sang again (Ezra 3:10-13), Zechariah and Haggai had to take them to task for neglecting spiritual matters. They were so blinded by "traditions" that when Christ came unto His own, "they received him not." Even till this day they are blinded in part. This is the record preserved for us of those "chosen by God" above all nations (Deut. 14:2) — of those who were entrusted with His sacred oracles (Rom. 3:2).

In spite of her dismal failure as a nation, there was a "faithful remnant" among the people, and because this nucleus remained true, God preserved the Hebrews (Isa. 1:9, 10). All that we find written about Israel was written "for our learning" (Rom. 15:4). What happened to them are examples or object lessons to us, to exhort and warn us not to do the same things. Their conduct was recorded so we could know what they did and profit by their deeds, both good and evil, and also that we might be encouraged to be numbered among the "faithful remnant" in these last days before the Lord returns (I Cor. 10:11).

240. *Decree of Artaxerxes*

CHAPTER SIX

The People Who Hid the Dead Sea Scrolls

Daniel's interpretation of Nebuchadnezzar's dream focuses our attention on four world empires from the time of Israel's captivity to the coming of her Messiah. They are: (1) Babylonian, which conquered Israel, under Nebuchadnezzar (No. 224); (2) Medo-Persian, which conquered Babylon and set Israel free, under Cyrus and Darius (No. 232); (3) Grecian, after Israel had resettled in the land, under Alexandria the Great (*No. 241*); and (4) Roman. This, of course, made Israel under Gentile domain.

241. Alexander the Great

Alexander conquered the then-known world and wept because there were no other worlds to conquer. When he died at the age of thirty-three, his kingdom was divided among several of his generals. By 168-164 B.C., Antiochus Epiphanes IV, king of Syria (*No. 242*), sought to bring the Jews under the sway of Grecian culture and religions. "For the king had sent letters . . . unto Jerusalem and the cities of Juda that they should follow the strange laws of the land

and pollute the sanctuary and holy people; set up altars and groves, chapels of idols, and to sacrifice swine's flesh and unclean beasts: that they also leave their children uncircumcised" (I Maccabees 1: 44-48). These crimes, which Antiochus IV added to his looting and desecration of the Temple in 168 B.C., sparked off rebellion and war under the leadership of the Maccabeans (three brothers — Judas, Simon, and Jonathan, with the nickname "Maccabeaus," meaning "the hammer"). After a series of brilliant victories, Jerusalem was liberated, and in 165 B.C., the Temple was cleansed and rededicated and pure worship was restored.

242. Antiochus Epiphanes

Due to a power vacuum in the Near East Israel enjoyed a century of political freedom. The Maccabean house was given the high priesthood of Israel, although by birth and training the family was not fitted for this office. As the line continued these priests became engaged more and more in Israel's wars and less engaged in religious matters. The moral deterioration of these priests helped to set the stage for the emergence of those who remained true to the old traditions of the priesthood. They soon found themselves in fierce opposition with the Jerusalem authorities, notably Jannaeus (103-76 B.C.). According to Josephus, a rebellion broke out among the opponents of Jannaeus. He pursued them, dragged them from their hiding places, and crucified at least eight hundred of them in Jerusalem.

In about 140 B.C. some priests fled the "city of blood" (Jerusalem) to the "city of Salt" (Qumran) in the desert near the Dead Sea. About 100 B.C. the leader, or "Teacher," of those who were true priests helped them establish their community, ordered their ways and inspired them with personal faith and hope. They became known as the "Essenes," and their purpose was fourfold: (1) to preserve the purity of the priesthood; (2) to hold to Moses, the Psalms, and the Prophets as their authority; (3) to practice their beliefs daily; and (4) to preserve the Word of God for their posterity. Having established themselves on the back side of the desert, Grecian power throughout the world was waning, and the fourth great world empire mentioned by Daniel was coming to the forefront. In 63 B.C., Pompey marched into Jerusalem, and the Roman legions put an end to the Jewish political freedom.

The Jews had such hatred for the Romans that by the late A.D. 60's rebellion was common throughout the land. All Jews became the enemy of Rome, and there was nothing left for Rome to do but crush them. This, of course, included the Essenes, simply because they were Jews. Even though they were trying to live a quiet life in the city of Salt (now called "Qumran"), they were in a

"cold war" with the corrupted priesthood in Jerusalem and in an impending "hot war" with the legionnaires of Rome. Troops under Vespasian (*No. 243*) were

243. Vespasian

in Jericho, barely seven miles away (Map, *No. 244*). When word of this reached the Essenes they no doubt had last minute prayers and then hid their sacred scrolls in caves overlooking the Dead Sea, hoping to escape to the desert (*No. 245*). They no doubt intended to return for their scrolls, but Vespasian's army captured their village in A.D. 68

244. Map of Qumran Region

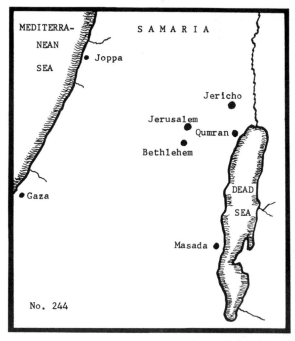

No. 244

245. *Judean Wilderness Near Dead Sea*

246. *Caves Near Qumran*

and evidentially wiped them out. This picture shows the general area of the Judean wilderness near the Dead Sea where the Essenes lived and hid their scrolls.

In 1947 a Judean wilderness shepherd-lad was looking for a stray goat at cliffs overlooking the Dead Sea, and noticed an opening over the edge. Throwing a rock at the "bull's eye," he heard a "ping" sound as the rock found its mark. Entering the cave (*No. 246,* arrow), he found a number of large jars (*No. 247*). Breaking some to find what he

247. *Broken Jars*

248. *Close-up of Caves*

thought would be gold, silver, and gems, he saw the ancient scrolls which the Essenes hid when Vespasian invaded their community 1,879 years before. *No. 248* is a close-up of one of the caves. This discovery startled the Biblical world, bringing to light portions of Scripture that had been written before Christ's day. Since 1947, portions of each book of the

249. *Leather Scroll, Linen, and Genesis Fragments*

Old Testament have been found except Esther. Probably Esther was excluded because of the late origin of the Feast of Purim.

Many scrolls were written on leather (*No. 249*) and were wrapped in linen (right). Fragments of Genesis are seen below the linen. A scroll which contained the complete book of Isaiah (*No. 250*) was found, along with many portions of Daniel, which indicated this book

250. *Isaiah Scroll*

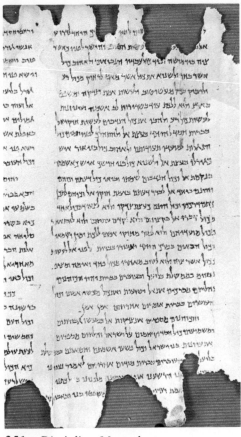

251. Discipline Manual

252. Copper Scrolls "in situ"

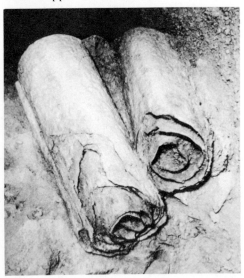

was also a favorite of the Essenes. A "commentary" on part of the book of Habakkuk was discovered. Their "Discipline" manual (*No. 251*) was among the many scrolls found intact, which informs us of the life and habits of the Essene community. It begins with the initiation rite for those who "enter the Covenant." Numerous non-Biblical scrolls were also discovered — a most popular one called the "Thanksgiving Hymn," which is similar to our Psalms. Bible critics were amazed to learn the Biblical scrolls read just like our King James Version, varying slightly, if any at all, in spelling or in copying from one of the scrolls to another. Scribes copied scrolls daily. The Isaiah scroll (No. 250) is the best preserved of all discovered. The total length is almost twenty-four feet. It contains seventeen sheets of parchment, approximately 15 x 10 inches, which were sewed together (left).

Copper scrolls, "in situ" (*No. 252*), were later opened. A special device (*No. 253*) was made to "saw" through each of them (*No. 254*). They were made of three strips of beaten copper, about eight feet in length and riveted together. There were twelve written columns which included a treasure record of gold and silver in bullion, coins and sacred vessels. No mention was made as to the location of these items, and the whereabouts of this vast hoard remains a mystery.

DATING THE SCROLLS

Of interest to the Christian is the way in which the scrolls have been dated. (1) Radio-carbon count dates the linen (No. 249), in which these scrolls were wrapped, from 175 B.C. to A.D. 225. (2) Paleography (style of writing). A leading archaeologist, W. F. Albright, has commented: "All competent students of writing conversant with the available

253. Copper Scroll

materials and with paleographic method date the scrolls in the 250 years before A.D. 70." (3) Pottery fragments as well as jars (No. 247), were of a type which was not produced after A.D. 100. (4) The copper sheets used for some scrolls (Nos. 252, 253) were characteristic of first-century metallurgy. (5) A cache of over five hundred silver coins (*No. 255*), which are first century B.C. and A.D. Another important discovery at Qumran helped excavators determine the date of the Essenes' existence at Qumran. An earthquake has been historically dated at 31 B.C. and its evidence is seen leading down the ceremonial

254. Opening a Scroll

255. Cache of Coins

stairway (*No. 256*). The ruins have further revealed over one thousand bowls from their kitchen, a "scriptorium" (writing room) with the remains of desks made of plaster and dried-out ink wells, fourteen different reservoirs, pools and baths, and an intricate system of viaducts. One pool measured fifty by fifteen feet. The Essenes were immersionists, undergoing baptismal rites often. Probably John the Baptist, son of a (spiritual) priest, was acquainted with these Essenes. Luke tells us he ". . . was in the deserts till the day of his showing unto Israel" (1:80).

The ancient Jewish fortress of Masada, south of Qumran, was recently excavated, and discoveries confirm an account by Josephus, "The War of the Jews." Josephus reported that members of a religious sect, Sicarri, before committing mass suicide, set fire to the compound, sparing only the food stores to let the Roman army know that they had not given up due to a lack of food. Excavations show all was destroyed except the food stores. Ruins of city buildings, covered with rich frescoes, support the account of Josephus that "floors and edifices were paved with stones in many colors." In a chasm 620 feet below, a compound was probed, which corresponds to the "caverns" described by Josephus. It was here two women and five children escaped from a massacre and lived to tell of the heroic fate of the defenders. Probably the most important discovery at Masada was broken pottery and a piece of papyrus inscribed in Hebrew which was the same script used by the scribes at Qumran. It is dated A.D. 73 or earlier.

THE EFFECT OF THE SCROLLS ON CHRISTIAN FAITH

Prior to the discovery of the "Dead Sea Scrolls," the oldest known manuscript of the Hebrew Old Testament was dated A.D. 826. We now have portions of the Old Testament that date back to 150 B.C., possibly to 200 B.C. This archaeological find has greater significance to the Biblical scholar than almost any other discovery in the last one hundred years.

Some "authorities" seem to think the scrolls challenge the uniqueness of Christ and Christian doctrine, because some things which characterize Christianity also characterized the Essenes. They claim that John the Baptist, Christ, and the early disciples took their ideas from those who lived at Qumran. There are some points of similarity but these do not necessarily prove dependency. There was the sharing of common goods, consideration of the poor, the sharing of common meals and baptism by immersion. Those at Qumran observed baptism as a purifying rite. None of the Essenes could be baptized until the applicant passed two years probation. The Jews themselves used baptism as a rite for admitting Gentile converts. With John and the early church, baptism was for *all* who repented, Jew and Gentile alike, and was observed immediately upon one's confession of faith in Christ (Acts 19:4; 8:35-39).

Possibly the most "serious" questions raised by these scrolls relate to the Person of Christ. Two of the documents mention (a few times) a Teacher of Righteousness. Nothing is known of his origin, the nature of his death, or even his name. He was not the founder of the Essenes, but was accepted as the teacher, and quite a few assumed that he was the "Prophet" (Deut. 18:18). However, he is never referred to or alluded to as the Messiah. There is no reference to his birth (much less of a virgin birth), none to the way he taught (parables or otherwise). If he was re-

256. *Earthquake Evidence*

sponsible for any of the writings of the Essenes, we are safe in saying his Biblical teachings were vastly different from Christ's. No miracles are ascribed to him and no disciples of his are mentioned. If the Essene officers are to be taken as the teacher's "apostles," then their duties were much different from this office as described in the New Testament. There is brief mention of this teacher's death, but no indication of resurrection or ascension. There is virtually no information concerning the "Teacher of Righteousness" or anything in any of the Dead Sea Scrolls that would, *in any way,* bring into question the uniqueness of the Lord Jesus Christ.

No truth of the Christian faith in these scrolls differs from what we find in the King James Version of the Bible. Christ read from an Isaiah scroll (Luke 4:16-21), and read what we read in our own Bibles. When we quote the Word of God we quote the same truths as Christ when He referred to the Scriptures. What difference we find in the Biblical scrolls

is minute. Our King James Version says "waters of Dimon" in Isaiah 15:9. The "Isaiah Scroll" says "waters of Dibon." The King James Version says "crooked places straight" and the Isaiah Scroll says "hills straight" (Isa. 45:2). The King James Version says "pour down righteousness" and the Isaiah Scroll says "rain down righteousness" (Isa. 45:8). Agreement between the "Isaiah Scroll," the Hebrew text of A.D. 826, and the text of our King James Version shows the care with which the scribes of old copied Bible manuscripts. "Isaiah" *is* still the same book it was when it came from the pen of the prophet Isaiah over twenty-seven hundred years ago.

For almost two thousand years the silence of the priesthood of Qumran verified the truth that all flesh is as grass, and that the glory of man fades away. But out of those Qumran caves has come further demonstration of the fact that although the grass withers and men die, the Word of God abides forever! (See I Peter 1:24, 25.)

CHAPTER SEVEN

New Testament Archaeology

The Old Testament covers a period of well over 4000 years. The last 2000 begins with the Patriarchs and its history ends with the record of Nehemiah and the prophecy of Malachi (ca. 400 B.C.). Between the end of the Old Testament period and the beginning of the New Testament era is a span of approximately 400 years, called the *"Inter-testamental Period."* Several important events took place during this time — the rise of the Grecians, whose language and culture swept the world of that day under the conquests of Alexander the Great, and the overthrow of the Greek empire by the Romans (the fourth great world empire of Daniel's vision) in 146 B.C., who ruled before, during, and after the New Testament period until A.D. 476. Because of the influence of Grecian culture even during the Roman period, its empire was known as the *"Graeco-Roman"* world.

The Inter-testamental Period produced many writings and groups or sects. Chapter 6 tells of the Essenes and their "Dead Sea Scrolls." The *"Apocrypha,"* a name given to fourteen books, originated during this time. These books were never in the Hebrew Old Testament canon, were not recognized as Scripture by the Jews, never referred to by Christ, nor accepted by the New Testament writers and early Church Fathers. The *"Pseudepigrapha"* were religious compositions written between 200 B.C. and A.D. 200 by authors who attributed them to many well-known Old Testament characters, and were primarily legendary.

The *"Targums"* were renderings of the Old Testament Scriptures into Aramaic when this language became common in Palestine after Israel's exile in Babylon. The *"Talmud"* is a compilation of Hebrew civil and canonical laws based on the Torah (Law) of Moses. It was the thinking or interpretation of these laws of Rabbis from about 300 B.C. to A.D. 500.

The *"Synagogue,"* which plays such an important role in the life of the Jews in the New Testament period, had its beginning, in all probability, in homes in Babylon while Israel was in captivity (Ezek. 8:1; 20:1-3). After their exile, scattered Jews, who could no longer go to Jerusalem for Temple worship, erected synagogues for worship, instruction in the Law, Psalms and Prophets, and prayer. Practically every town where Jews lived in numbers from 300 B.C. to A.D. 300 had its own synagogue (cf. Luke 4:44). The synagogues became the storehouses for the Hebrew Scriptures and were among the first places where early New Testament saints proclaimed the gospel (Acts 9:20; 13:5).

Other sects which came to the forefront during this period, and were in existence in early New Testament days, were: (1) the *Pharisees,* who stood true to the Law of Moses when Antiochus Epiphanes sought to destroy all traces of Judaism in 168 B.C. They were legalistic separatists who, by Christ's day, had become mere religionists and had substituted the traditions of their fathers for the Scriptures. (2) The *Sadducees* were rationalistic or worldly-minded priests who obeyed the letter of the Law but conformed to Graeco-Roman culture. Although they were opponents of the

Pharisees and denied the resurrection and future judgment, they assisted the Pharisees in their opposition to Christ. (3) The *Scribes,* whose task was to copy the Scriptures, were fully versed in the Law. They were also called *"Lawyers."* Many political groups arose during this time, especially prior to and during the life of Christ. Two among them were the *Herodians,* who sought to perpetuate the Herods on the throne, and the *Zealots,* who wanted no foreign ruler.

The *"Sanhedrin,"* whose beginning probably originated in the days of King Jehoshaphat (II Chron. 19:4-11), was chiefly the "Supreme Court" of Jesus' day, and judged both civil and religious matters until Jerusalem's fall in A.D. 70. It was made up of seventy members, and was presided over by the High Priest.

A most important writing in this period was the *"Septuagint."* After the Exile, many Jews were dispersed in all parts of the Graeco-Roman world. Living among pagans, the ancient people of God won many proselytes to Judaism. With Greek being the common language, there was a need for a Greek translation of the Hebrew Scriptures. Under the direction of Ptolemy II of Egypt, the High Priest of Jerusalem was requested to permit this translation, and it was completed on the Island of Pharos off Alexandria (285-130 B.C.).

It can be said that "Greek learning and culture, Roman law and Roman roads, Jewish monotheism and Jewish synagogues (the latter widespread as a result of the Jewish diaspora), and Jewish apocalyptic and messianic hopes prepared the world for the coming of Christ and Christianity. Divine providence can be traced everywhere in the long interval between the Testaments. The goal was the incarnation and birth of the long-awaited Messiah and Saviour of the world, prophesied so often in the Old Testament. To this great event all preceding centuries of world history, especially Jewish history, pointed" (*Unger's Bible Handbook.* Used by permission, Moody Press, Moody Bible Institute of Chicago).

However, the life of Christ itself offers very little that has left material evidence buried beneath the ruins of time. He built no palaces, nor temples, nor cities, neither had victorious campaigns nor destroyed and burned cities and countrysides. The archaeologists have had to reconstruct His environment and rediscover villages where He lived and worked and preached, and died. From both the Gospel accounts of Matthew, Mark, Luke, and John and records and buildings left by the Greeks and Romans, have come sufficient evidence to substantiate the claims of those who still believe the Bible record. This holds true for cities and places mentioned in Paul's missionary journeys, and other events recorded in the book of Acts. The best guide for archaeologists has been many ancient copies of the New Testament, which are only a few decades removed from the time of Christ.

Yet the critic of the Word still raises his voice. Such a critic was Sir William M. Ramsay, who doubted the historicity of the book of Acts. He claimed it was written the latter part of the second century. Paid by the British Museum to do research work in ancient Grecian lands and Asia Minor, he found no maps that could be trusted. Turning to the New Testament to learn of cities that existed then, he took Acts 14:5, 6 as his starting point and discovered an inscription in the area mentioned which contradicted the critics of his day, who said that Iconium was located in Lycaonia and not in Phrygia. Ramsay learned that Luke's statement in Acts was accurate. Ramsay also held the critic's view that

257. *Caesar Augustus*

Galatia was in northern Asia Minor, but after an examination of some inscriptions concluded Luke was correct in his historical and geographical knowledge of his day — that Galatia *was* in the southern district, and included such cities as Antioch, Iconium, Derbe, and Lystra. He was so impressed with these facts (and many others) that he became an ardent advocate of the historicity of the book of Acts.

W. J. Conybeare, late Fellow of Trinity College, Cambridge, England, was a scholar and critic who did not believe the claims of Christ nor the teachings of the Jews concerning God. He went to Palestine to write a record that would prove their fallacy. As a result of his studies of evidence at hand, he accepted Christ as his own personal Saviour and did his writings to prove that Jesus was the Redeemer of mankind.

Lew Wallace, an army officer and skeptic of some years ago, sought to discredit the claims of Christ through a study of the critic's "evidence," but found such overwhelming evidence to the contrary that he arrived at the conclusion that Christ was truly the Son of God, the founder of Christianity, and wrote the classic, "Ben Hur," a story of a believer in Christ under Roman rule.

Simon Greenleaf, a great American lawyer of the past, wrote one of the most important works on the law of evidence ever to appear in the English language — "A Treatise on the Law of Evidence." He also wrote a volume in which he examined the testimony of the four Gospel accounts of Christ. He applied the same laws of evidence as used in courts, and said, "Our profession leads us to explore the mazes of falsehood, to detect its artifices, to pierce its thickest veils, to follow and expose its sophistries, to compare the statements of different witnesses with severity, to discover truth and separate it from error." He came to the conclusion that the four Gospels are absolutely trustworthy, and that the four writers could not have lied about Christ, for their testimony most emphatically rings true.

THE LIFE OF CHRIST

"And it *came* to pass in those days, that there went out a decree from Caesar Augustus [*No. 257*], that all the world should be taxed. (And this taxing was first made when Cyrenius was governor of Syria.) And all went to be taxed, everyone into his own city" (Luke 2: 1-3). This decree necessitated Mary and Joseph's journey from Nazareth to Bethlehem, where the babe Christ was born in fulfillment of the prophecy uttered by Micah (5:2; Luke 2:3-5).

Critics of this account by Luke accused him of making five errors. (1) That Cyrenius was not governor of Syria at this time, but later. (2) That Augustus never ordered a census. (3) That there wasn't any such system of taking

258. *Caesar's Podium*

a census. (4) That if there was a census, it would not be necessary for one to go to his own city, and (5) that if the husband went, it wasn't necessary for the wife to make the journey. It was Sir William M. Ramsay who proved by several inscriptions that Quirinius (or Cyrenius) was twice governor of Syria — the first time when Christ was born, and the second time at a later date. Egyptian papyri also supports Luke's record, indicating that a census was taken every fourteen years. The cycle of these enrollments shows the approximate date of the one recorded by Luke was 6-5 B.C., which is accepted as the date of Christ's birth. (Our calendar today, which starts with His birth, is off by several years.) Other papyrus documents mention "Tiberius Claudius Caesar Augustus Germanicus Emperor" by name, and also

support Luke's claim regarding one's journey to his homeland to pay his taxes *with* his household. The podium from which Augustus made his decree is still seen today in the old Roman Forum (*No. 258*).

While Mary and Joseph were in Bethlehem, "the days were accomplished that she should be delivered. And she brought forth her firstborn son, and wrapped him in swaddling clothes, and laid him in a manger; because there was no room for them in the inn" (Luke 2:6, 7). Mangers (*No. 259*) are still used today in the Holy Land as a crib or trough for feeding animals.

Very little is said in the New Testament about Christ between His birth and when He was a young boy twelve years old. As the "child Christ" He was taken to the Temple to be presented to the

259. *Manger*

260. *The Temple Site*

Lord (Luke 2:21-39). Herod's decree
that all males two years and under
should be slaughtered brought about the
flight of Mary and Joseph and the "young
child" into Egypt (Matt. 2:13-23). The
"child" grew and at the age of twelve He
was taken to the Passover in Jerusalem
where, being "about His Father's business," confounded the doctors of His day
(Luke 2:40-49). *No. 260* is the Temple
site where these events occurred.

The only thing said about Christ between the ages of twelve and thirty is
that He "increased in wisdom and stature,
and in favor with God and man" (Luke
2:52—3:23). At the beginning of His
earthly ministry, He was met by John,
who introduced Him as "the lamb of God
who taketh away the sin of the world"
(John 1:29). Baptized by John in the

river Jordan, He went into the wilderness
for forty days and was tempted by the
devil (Luke 4:1-13). *No. 261* is the
traditional site of Christ's baptism, and
No. 262 is the Mount of Temptation,
where Satan tempted Christ to bow down
and worship him.

After His wilderness experience, Christ
"returned in the power of the Spirit into
Galilee; and there went out a fame of
him throughout all the region round
about. And he taught in their synagogues . . ." (Luke 4:14-30). *No. 263*
shows the ruins of a synagogue at Capernaum, which was built over the site
of the one where Christ taught each Sabbath He was there (Luke 4:31-38a).
Not only did He mingle with the people
and teach the multitudes throughout the
countryside and those in attendance in

261. *Baptismal Site of Christ*

262. *Mount of Temptation*

263. *Ruins of Synagogue at Capernaum*

264. *Jacob's Well*

265. *Samaritan and Scroll*

the synagogues, but He was vitally interested in individuals as well. One such incident was His encountering a woman at Jacob's well as He passed through Samaria. This well (*No. 264*) is still in use today near the little village of Sycar, and it was here that Christ revealed Himself as Messiah (John 4:4-42).

After the Northern Kingdom of Israel fell and its captives were taken to other areas controlled by the Assyrians, the land was resettled by those who later became known as "Samaritans" (p. 136). They were never accepted by the Jews who returned from captivity (Ezra 4:1-10). During the days of Christ, the Jews and Samaritans were still at odds — the Jews having "no dealings with the Samaritans" (John 4:9). Samaritans still exist today in the Near East, their number being several hundred. Once a year they offer the "Passover Lamb" on mount Gerazim, which is in plain view of Jacob's well. *No. 265* shows a present-day high priest of the Samaritans with an ancient scroll which they claim was written by Aaron's grandson. It contains only the Pentateuch. This is the only divinely inspired portion of Scripture to them; the rest of the Old Testament is merely historical.

179

266. *Farthings and Penny*

267. *Millstones*

First Century coins of Palestine were made of three metals — gold, silver, and copper. Christ referred to these three varieties when He told his disciples, "Provide neither gold, nor silver, nor brass [copper] in your purses" (Matt. 10:9). Many Greek and Roman coins have been discovered and are of importance to the archaeologist because they preserve for us the likeness of dignitaries, temples and buildings which have been inscribed on them. Some Greek coins have been found that bear the likeness of the goddess Diana and her Temple at Ephesus (p. 196). Christ used a coin to illustrate God's love to those who know Him: "Are not two sparrows sold for a farthing?" (Matt. 10:29-31). Farthings (*No. 266,* upper coins), are worth about one-quarter cent each. When the Herodians sought to trap Jesus regarding lawful payment of taxes, they brought Him a penny at His request, which contained the image and superscription of Caesar (Matt. 22:15-22; No. 266, lower coin). These are Roman coins made of copper. (The "farthing" was called *Quadrans* and the "penny" was called *Denarius.*) The *Stater* ("a piece of money" — Matt. 17:27) was the coin that Peter found in

the mouth of a fish. It was a Greek coin, made of an alloy of gold mixed with silver, and was the Temple-tax for Jesus and Peter. The *Didrachma* ("tribute" or "half-shekel") was also a Greek coin, the value of which paid the Temple-tax for one person (Matt. 17:24). The *Drachma* ("piece of silver") was the Greek coin lost by a woman (Luke 15:8). This coin was worth half the value of the didrachma. The *Lepton* ("mite") was a Greek copper coin, the smallest of Palestinian coins, and was worth about one-eighth of a cent. A widow gave "two mites" as Christ observed those who cast their gifts into the treasury (Luke 21:1-4). See No. 66 for the "widow's mites."

One form of capital punishment practiced by the Greeks and Romans was the tying of millstones (*No. 267*) around the necks of the condemned and casting them into the sea. To impress upon His hearers the importance of setting a good example before little children, Christ said that if one offended any of the little ones who had come to Him, "It were better for him that a millstone were hanged about his neck and . . . drowned in the depth of the sea" (Matt. 18:1-6).

268. *Sepulchres*

269. *House of Mary and Martha*

270. *Tomb of Lazarus*

271. *Boundary Stone*

The "common people" heard Christ gladly (Mark 12:37b), and this was a blow to the proud Pharisees, who displayed their religion publicly (Matt. 6: 2, 5; 23:5-7). They bitterly opposed Christ and His teachings and plotted often to take His life. He, in turn, condemned them for their life of legalism and hypocrisy. They were classified as a "generation of vipers" (Matt. 23:33), upbraided for their pride and self-righteousness (Matt. 9:10-13), taken to task for their misunderstanding of the meaning of the Sabbath (Matt. 12:1-8), rebuked for not having submitted to baptism (Luke 7:30-35), condemned for their covetousness (Luke 16:13-15), labeled "blind guides," and called hypocrites of the highest order (Matt. 23:13-36). To illustrate their hypocrisy, Christ likened them to "whited sepulchres [*No. 268*], which indeed appear beautiful outward, but are within full of dead men's bones, and of all uncleanness" (Matt. 23:27, 28).

Jesus often visited and lodged in Bethany with His friends (Matt. 21:17; 26:6; John 12:1, 2). His disciples were sent from Bethany to fetch a colt for Him to ride into Jerusalem (Mark 11:1-11), and that same night He returned to this little village. It was the home of His dear friends, Mary, Martha and Lazarus. *No. 269* shows the ruins of their house as seen today in Bethany. *No. 270* is the entrance to the reputed tomb of Lazarus where Jesus cried with a loud voice, saying, "Lazarus, come forth," and raised him from the dead (John 11: 1-44). Bethany was on the other side of the mount of Olives east of Jerusalem, and was considered a "Sabbath day's journey" from one to the other. *No. 271* is an inscribed stone in a field which denotes the end of such a journey (Acts 1:12).

No. 272 shows lamps and oil cruses, the type which Christ had in mind when

272. *Lamps and Oil Cruses*

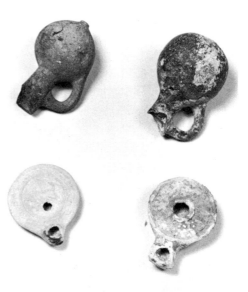

273. *Triumphal Entry Gate*

He illustrated readiness in the parable of the Ten Virgins (Matt. 25:1-13). These lamps fit easily in the palm of one's hand. The five "wise" virgins, who had an extra supply of oil in a small cruse, would replenish their lamps by pouring olive oil into the center opening. The extra supply of oil illustrates one's readiness for Christ's soon return. (See No. 23 for "mill" — Matt. 24:41, which was also used by Christ to illustrate preparation for His second coming.)

From the ushering in of Christ's earthly ministry to the entrance of His last week before His crucifixion, Luke tells us that God had anointed Him with power, and that He went about doing good, healing all that were oppressed of the devil; for God was with Him (Acts 10:38). He had often told His disciples that He must go to Jerusalem and die (Matt. 16:21; 20:28). It had been prophesied of Him that for the purpose of His coming into the world He would "set his face as a flint" to the task (Isa. 50:6, 7). His hour is now about upon Him and preparation is made for this last week. The first move was His "triumphal entry" into Jerusalem (Matt. 21:1-11). *No. 273* is the sealed gate at the site where Christ entered into the city. The colt (No. 180)

reminds us of the one He rode on this occasion. (Ezekiel prophesied this gate would be sealed *after* the Lord God of Israel [Christ incarnate] had entered in by it: 44:1, 2. It is also the site where Peter and John healed the lame man at the gate called "Beautiful" when on their way to the Temple to pray: Acts 3:1-10.)

The "Garden of Gethsemane" (foreground, No. 273) is where Christ prayed, and was later betrayed by Judas (Matt. 26:36-50). Judas had previously bargained with the chief priests to deliver Christ into their hands, saying to them, "What will ye give to me, and I will deliver Him unto you? And they cove-

274. *Silver Coins*

275. *Pilate Stone and Coins*

276. *Roman Game*

nanted with him for 30 pieces of silver" (Matt. 26:14-16; 27:3-10). *No. 274* shows some silver coins, the type Judas received for his infamous act. By now Christ had been arrested, and after some political maneuvering, faced trial before Pontius Pilate, was condemned to death, scourged, and sent on His way bearing the cross to be crucified (John 18:12-14, 19—19:17). There have been those who doubted the existence of Pilate, but an inscription bearing the name "Pontius Pilate" found at Caesarea and coins which had been minted in his honor in A.D. 30-31 bear testimony to the truthfulness of the Gospel accounts regarding Pilate in the life of Christ (*No. 275*). While the drama of the ages was in progress before Pilate, Roman soldiers, indifferent to its significance, played games. *No. 276* is an old Roman game carved in the pavement beneath Pilate's judgment hall.

277. *Via Dolorosa*

278. *Damascus Gate*

After Christ was scourged and condemned to death, He bore the cross to Calvary. The "Via Dolorosa" (*No. 277*) shows part of the pavement where Christ stood before Pilate, and over which He made his way to Golgotha (Matt. 27:26-33). The "Damascus Gate" (*No. 278*) is over the site of the gate through which Christ made His exit from Jerusalem to suffer outside the gate (Heb. 13:12).

279. *The Place of Skull — Golgotha*

The place of the "skull" (*No. 279*) is where Christ hung between two thieves and bore in His body our sins (Mark 15: 22, 27; I Peter 2:24). When Jesus yielded up the ghost, the veil of the Temple was rent in twain from the top to the bottom; and the earth did quake, and the rocks rent (Matt. 27:45-51). *No. 280 is* a view looking toward Jerusalem from Calvary, showing some earthquake evidence — where the "rocks rent."

After Jesus died, and the authorities were sure of His death, Joseph of Arimathaea, being a disciple of Jesus, besought Pilate that he might take away the body of Jesus. This request was granted,

280. *Earthquake near Calvary*

281. Tomb of Joseph

and Joseph was assisted by Nicodemus in taking down the body and preparing it for burial. Joseph owned a newly hewn tomb in a garden near where Christ's crucifixion took place, and it was here that He was buried *(No. 281.* See John 19:38-42, and also "Rolling Stone" No. 218).

Christ had predicted He would be raised the third day after he was killed (Matt. 16:21; John 2:19-21). The chief priests and Pharisees remembered this saying and commanded of Pilate that the sepulchre be made sure until the third day. They were given a watch (guards) and the tomb was sealed (Matt. 27:62-66). An inscription *(No. 282),* said to have been found in Nazareth in 1878, reveals an "ordinance of Caesar" demanding trial of anyone who "has in any way extracted the buried or maliciously transferred them to another place . . . or has displaced the sealing or other stones." This ordinance, called the "Nazareth De-

282. Nazareth Decree

283. The Empty Tomb

cree" or "Tomb Robbers' Inscription," could possibly explain one of the reasons why a watch was set at Christ's tomb and why it was sealed. The guards' efforts were in vain, for God sent an earthquake and rolled away the sealed stone from the tomb, revealing the fulfillment of Christ's prediction. When His followers visited the tomb on the third day, they were greeted by an angel, who told them, "He is not here," and instructed them to "Come, see the place where the Lord lay" (No. 283. See Matt. 28:1-6). "Up from the grave He arose, with a mighty triumph o'er His foes." Even the "watch" was baffled at His resurrection (Matt. 28:11-15).

Christ's resurrection was God's victory over sin and hell and death (I Cor. 15:17; Rev. 1:5, 18). His resurrection made possible His leading or taking captive the one who formerly had held captive those in bondage of sin and in fear of death — "He led captivity captive" (Eph. 4:8; Heb. 2:14, 15). Through the mighty working of God's power in resurrection, Christ is now above all principality, and power, and might, and dominion, and every name that is named . . . and hath . . . all things under His feet (Eph. 1:20-22). Paul used the ancient custom of victorious monarchs who had images of defeated foes carved on their footstools to illustrate this truth regarding Christ. No. 284 is the footstool of king Tut-ankh-amun of Egypt, showing images of his defeated enemies on the top and sides.

284. King Tut's Footstool

285. *Earliest Crucifix*

Before Christ was crucified, He predicted that after His ascension His followers would be persecuted and many would have to forfeit their lives in defense of the gospel (Matt. 24:9). The spark that urged the disciples to faithfully proclaim Christ was their living hope in a living Saviour. This became their theme in the book of Acts. Under persecution they said they "should obey God rather than men" and rejoiced "that they were counted worthy to suffer shame for his name" (Acts 5:29, 40-42). This theme of the living Christ continued from one generation to another as they earnestly contended for the faith. In the midst of severe persecution, which saw multitudes of Christians slain for their refusal to deny Christ as their Saviour, these saints never thought of God's Son as a *dying* Saviour, nailed to a cross, dead — but alive forevermore! As Christianity became "accepted" and then later adopted as a state religion, less emphasis was placed on the risen Lord and more emphasis on His death. *No. 285* is a picture of the earliest known Crucifix, which is on an engraved gem of the fourth century.

It was mentioned earlier in this chapter that Christ Himself left very little material evidence concerning His earthly life. Since critics are quick to grab at any straw in the wind that would fortify their position, they claimed that the New Testament *only* contained a record of Christ, and that if He had really lived, historians of the Roman period would have included Him in their writings. Archaeological evidence has been swift to refute their argument. Tacitus, in recording the persecution of Nero, mentions that Christians derived their name "from one Christus, who was executed in the reign of Tiberius by the procurator of Judaea, Pontius Pilate." Josephus, Celsus, and Lucian the Cynic also mentioned Christ in their writings. Pliny the Younger wrote to Emperor Trajan regarding treatment of Christians. He testified of their piety and allegiance to their founder, Christ. To these testi-

286. *Damascus Wall and House*

monies can be added those of the early Church Fathers, early Christian writings, old Jewish texts, and many hymns and articles found in Egypt. It has been difficult indeed for the critic to prove the non-existence of Jesus Christ.

THE LIFE OF PAUL

The main source for the life of Paul is Luke's account in the book of Acts, with added information from Paul's own letters. He was born of purest Jewish blood in the Graeco-Roman city of Tarsus in Cilicia, possibly about the time of Christ's birth, and was named Saul. His birth in Tarsus made him a Roman citizen (Phil. 3:5; Acts 21:39; 22:25-28). This city was a noted trading center, and was known particularly for its manufacture of goats' hair cloth. It was here that young Saul learned his trade of tentmaking (Acts 18:3). The Greek geographer, Strabo, mentions this great city as having a university to rival those of Athens and Alexandria. Athenodorus, the philosopher, who was the famous teacher of the Emperor Augustus, was a native of Tarsus. An inscription calls Tarsus "the great and wondrous metropolis of Cilicia."

He was reared in orthodox Judaism as the son of a Pharisee (Acts 23:6), and later sent to Jerusalem to complete his studies under Gamaliel (Acts 22:3; 26:4, 5). As a student he was second to none and became a zealous "Hebrew of the Hebrews" and a Pharisee (Gal. 1:14; Phil. 3:4-6). His zeal for the Law gave him leadership in Judaism, and his first public appearance recorded in Acts was that of supervising the stoning of Stephen, followed by great persecution against the Church (Acts 7:58—8:3; 9:1, 2). Acts 26:10, 11 reveal his fanatical devotion to the Jews' religion. He believed he was God's anointed to destroy the Church (Acts 26:9), although he acted in ignorant unbelief (I Tim. 1:13).

While on a journey from Jerusalem to Damascus to arrest Christians, Saul was arrested by Jesus, and was gloriously converted to Christianity (Acts 9:1-16). Having been blinded by a light from heaven, he was led into Damascus where his sight was later restored. "And straightway he preached Christ in the synagogues, that he is the Son of God" (Acts 9:20). The Jews turned on him

*287. Temple
Warning
against Greeks*

and sought to do to him what he had been doing to other followers of Christ. He was befriended by the disciples there, who probably knew someone who lived in a house on the city wall, and saved his life by letting him down "by the wall in a basket" (Acts 9:21-25). *No. 286* shows a section of the ancient wall of Damascus of Paul's day.

It will be noted in the book of Acts that when Paul entered a city to preach Christ, he usually headed for the synagogue first, to reason with the Jews. When he finished with them, he would turn to the Gentiles, who were waiting in an outer court of the synagogue. This was the custom of that day, and is one reason why Paul went to the Jew first and then to the Gentile second (Acts 13:14, 15, 42). No. 263 shows the gathering place of the Jews in a synagogue. An inscription stone from Herod's Temple (*No. 287*) forbade any Gentile to enter the Jewish section of the Temple or synagogue under penalty of death. This also confirms the enmity between Jews and Gentiles (John 4:9; Mark 7:25-30). *No. 288* is the "Seat of Moses"

288. Seat of Moses

289. *Inscription of Luke's Day*

(Matt. 23:2), a special seat in the synagogue for the principle teacher. Paul, no doubt, often sat in such seats in their synagogues as he reasoned with the Jews concerning the Scriptures.

Archaeology sheds light on the "great dearth throughout all the world," which stirred the Christians in Antioch to send help by Paul to the suffering saints in Jerusalem (Acts 11:27-30). Ramsay collected evidence to show that this famine did in fact exist. It is recorded by two Roman writers, Cassius and Tacitus, that there were bad harvests in Asia Minor and the Mediterranean area, and that Claudius decreed famine prices for food at that time. While the famine was announced by divine revelation to Agabus, it literally took place as attested to by secular history and was referred to later by Paul when he wrote to those in Galatia (Gal. 2:1-10).

In mentioning names and titles of those whom Paul encountered in his travels, critics have concluded that Luke was in error in his use of Greek words. Many first century Greek texts are in existence, but most of them are written in classical Greek. This differs from the New Testament language, and a number of scholars had a field day. The Greek of the papyri discovered in Egypt was different, and soon a comparison revealed it to be a vernacular Greek used in the Near East — Greek as it was spoken and written by the common people of that day. It *was* the language found in the New Testament, and accounts for the use of many words and expressions not found in manuscripts of the first century which used classical Greek.

As an example, Cyprus was annexed by Rome and in a period of thirty-five years had four types of Roman government, each ruled over by a "titled" officer. Because Luke was well acquainted with these facts, it was hardly likely he would use the wrong title. In Acts 13:7 he uses the correct title of "deputy," which would not have appeared in classical Greek. He also used correctly the expression "chief man" of the island of Malta where Paul was shipwrecked (Acts 28:7). This is confirmed by two Maltese inscriptions, one in Greek and the other in Latin. Another such example of Luke's accuracy is shown in the Greek inscription (*No. 289*) which was once a part of the Gate of Vardar at Thessalo-

290. *Old Market Place — Athens*

nica, listing six "politarchs," which is the common Greek word for "rulers of the city," used by him in Acts 17:6.

Much of Paul's action in Acts centers around his missionary journeys. Running true to form in his determination to know nothing among men "save Jesus Christ and Him crucified" (I Cor. 2:2), he entered Athens, reasoned with the Jews in the synagogue, and approached those from all walks of life in the market (Acts 17:17). *No. 290* shows the ruins of the old market place in Athens where Paul witnessed daily of his resurrected Lord. It seemed as though this Apostle to the Gentiles was doubly concerned for the Athenians, for "his spirit was stirred in him, when he saw the city wholly given to idolatry" (Acts 17:16). *No. 291* is such a scene witnessed by Paul — idols of "stone, graven by árt and man's device" (Acts 17:29).

291. *Athenian Gods*

292. Seats of Philosophers

Among the groups of philosophers who lived in Athens, two were the self-sufficient Epicureans and the Stoics, who daily sat in amphitheatre seats (*No. 292*) discussing avenues of approach in their pursuit of happiness and also seeking "to hear some new thing" (Acts 17:18-21). Since Paul's arrival in Athens they had heard the "new thing" concerning Jesus and the resurrection. They took him to the Areopagus (Mars' hill — knoll in center, *No. 293*) to learn of this new doctrine. Here Paul preached his famous sermon as is recorded in Acts 17:22-31. The Acropolis in the background shows the Parthenon, probably the temple "made with hands" to which he referred (vs. 24). While being taken to Mars' hill, Paul observed their devotions, and noticed an altar with this inscription, TO THE UNKNOWN GOD (Acts 17:23). The Greeks were polytheistic — having a god for any and every thing (No. 291). Paul told them "that in all things ye are too superstitious" (very religious). Not only did their many idols and temples prove this, but for fear of overlooking a god or goddess, they erected altars to unknown divinities (*No. 294*). This inscription says, "Sacred, whether it be to a god or goddess." Paul used their own device to tell them he *knew* their "unknown god."

Paul left Athens and began a work in Corinth. He became acquainted with Aquilla and Priscilla and stayed with them for the one and a half years he was in their city, working at his trade as a tentmaker. He reasoned with the Jews every Sabbath, persuading both Jews and Greeks that Jesus was the Christ. Finally, opposition arose among some Jews and they charged Paul with preaching a religion contrary to Roman law. He was brought before Gallio, the proconsul of Achaia (Acts 18:1-17). An inscription found in Delphi in 1908 bears the name of Gallio when he was in office.

293. *Mars' Hill*

294. *Altar to "Unknown God"*

A fragment of this inscription (*No. 295*) is seen, and from this discovery we are able to date Paul's visit to Corinth at about A.D. 51-53. When Paul wrote to the Corinthians several years later, remembering he had appeared before Gallio's judgment seat, he said in effect: "All might not have to appear before an earthly judge, but all must appear before the judgment seat of Christ" (II Cor. 5:10). *No. 296* shows the ruins of Gallio's "Bema" (or judgment seat) where Paul was tried.

296. Gallio's Bema   *295. Corinth Inscription*

297. *"Beating the Air"*

Corinth was a "sports-minded" city. Tarsus, too, was a city of sports, and much of this must have rubbed off on Paul. He often used sports to illustrate a spiritual truth. To encourage the Corinthians in their warfare against Satan, he referred to a technique in boxing to drive home his point: "So fight I, not as one that beateth the air" (I Cor. 9:26b, 27). A boxer disciplines himself and keeps his body under control, lest entering the ring unprepared, he swings his arms right and left hoping for a knockdown, but finds himself "beating the air," and is soon overcome by his opponent. Paul knew the value of spiritual discipline in spiritual warfare, and in the arena against the foe he wanted to aim every blow well and be triumphant in Christ (II Cor. 2:14). *No. 297* is a painting on a vase of Paul's day depicting a boxing match.

He also likened every believer as an athlete in the race of life (I Cor. 9:24-26a). Just as there is need for discipline lest we "beat the air," so the be-

298. *Victory Cup*

liever, as an athlete, must train if he is to be a winner. However, in the olympics, only one could win the race, and the prize was a corruptible crown (laurel wreath — p. 204, No. 316) or a victory cup (*No. 298*). But in the Christian

299. "Great is Diana"

This led to a two hour uproar in Ephesus (Acts 19). Archaeological evidence confirms this Biblical account of the religion of the Ephesians. *No. 299* is a statue of the multiple-breasted "Diana the Great," which symbolizes "fertility." The coin, struck in her honor, shows the head of the goddess and the cult image of this lewd religion. Excavations in Ephesus have given us information about her temple, which was one of the seven wonders of the ancient world. It was considered so holy that citizens of Ephesus as well as foreigners deposited their money in it for safekeeping. Gifts were made to the goddess, and one inscription tells of one V. Salutaris who gave twenty-nine gold and silver statues of Diana to be used in public processions. Her tem-

300. New Testament Era Letter

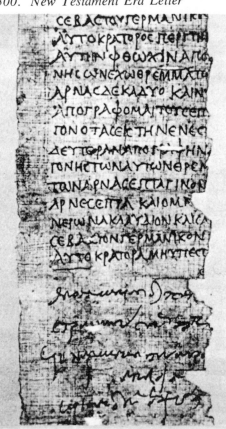

race, every believer can be a winner, receiving an "incorruptible crown." This crown, of course, goes only to those who so run — striving for the mastery and temperate in all things. The cup (No. 298) is inscribed: "Take the Victory."

In Ephesus Paul spoke boldly in the synagogue concerning the kingdom of God. The name of the Lord Jesus was magnified and many believed. As a result of their conversion, and the conversion of others throughout Asia under Paul's ministry, idol makers began to lose business, particularly Demetrius, a silversmith who made silver shrines for Diana, the goddess of the Ephesians.

301. A Sealed Epistle

ple was 180 x 377 feet. The roof was supported by 117 sixty-foot columns, and were six feet in diameter. A whole month each year was dedicated to the worship of this goddess, with such cries as, "Great is Diana of the Ephesians." The amphitheatre, scene of the riot and uproar of the silversmiths and worshipers of Diana which ensued because of the effect of Paul's ministry, was also found. It was 495 feet in diameter and could seat about 25,000.

Paul wrote thirteen Epistles to fellow-workers, acquaintances, and churches he helped to establish. (Some scholars are of the opinion he also wrote the book of Hebrews.) His letters were to encourage believers, straighten out church matters, and further explain truths he had taught while on his missionary journeys. His salutation "in his own handwriting" would be distinguishable from the style of his scribe. His Epistles often contained a word of personal greeting or salutation, and would look like this first century papyrus document (*No. 300.* See Colossians 4:18). *No. 301* shows how one of Paul's Epistles looked — tied and sealed — ready to be delivered by a messenger to the church or individual designated.

Soldiers played an important role in the lives of those who made up the Roman empire. *No. 302* is a monument of a Roman soldier capturing a prisoner to be sold into slavery. Paul's letter to Philemon had to do with a converted slave being a "brother" with his Christian master (Gal. 3:28). Approximately 30 per cent of Rome's population were slaves. *No. 303* shows Roman soldiers dressed in full armor, ready for battle.

302. Capturing a Slave

303. Whole Armor

Paul knew those at Ephesus would understand the following spiritual application, for such was a daily common sight; "Put on the whole armor of God — the belt of truth around your loins, . . . the breastplate of righteousness, . . . feet shod with the preparation of the gospel, . . . the shield of faith, . . . the helmet of salvation, and the sword of the Spirit, with prayer — to overcome the strategies of the devil" (Eph. 6:11-18).

Because of Paul's return to Jerusalem, he ran afoul of antagonistic Jews. Some plotted to take his life. Accusations were made against him and the Sanhedrin turned him over to Felix, the governor. Detained for two years in Caeserea, Paul later appeared before Festus. When Festus sought to use him to please the Jews, Paul, a Roman citizen, appealed to Caesar to state his case. Because there was no civil case against him, Festus permitted Agrippa to hear

304. *Agrippa*

305. *Village of Appii*

306. Roman Forum

Paul, thinking Agrippa might be able to solve the problem (Acts 21:14—25:27). In making his defense before Agrippa (*No. 304*), Paul related his conversion, stated his convictions, showed the courage of his convictions, and revealed his compassion for those who knew not Christ as Saviour. At the conclusion of his appeal, Agrippa said unto Festus, "This man might have been set at liberty, if he had not appealed unto Caesar" (Acts 26). See "Paul's boldness," p. 201.

Paul set sail for Rome from Caesarea, made stops at Myra in Asia Minor, Lasea on the island of Crete, the island of Malta, Syracuse in Sicily, and then finally arrived at Puteoli, below Naples, Italy. From there he made his way to Rome on foot, passing through the village of Appii (*No. 305*), where he was met by believers who had come down from Rome to greet him (Acts 27, 28). Arriving in Rome, he was to have made his defense before Caesar in the Roman Forum (*No. 306*). See "Caesar's Podium," No. 258.

There is a question whether Paul was imprisoned twice in Rome. Be that as it may, he was placed in the old Mamertine prison to await trial. Having been inside this prison myself (as a visitor!), I can appreciate his writing to Timothy

307. Mamertine
Prison

for his cloak (II Tim. 4:13). The plaque (*No. 307*), inside the prison, depicts Paul laying hands on newly won converts to Christ. This is where he wrote his "Prison Epistles" (Ephesians, Colossians, Philemon, Philippians, and Second Timothy).

The Caesar before whom Paul was to have stood was Nero (*No. 308*), who

308. Nero

charged the Christians with the burning of Rome (see p. 203 for an account of Nero's persecution of Christians). Because of his hatred for the followers of Christ, he ordered many of them crucified as their Saviour had been. But Paul was a Roman citizen, and Nero commanded him to be beheaded. This was

done about A.D. 66 or early 67. Paul's parting words at the close of his earthly life were: "For I am now ready to be offered, and the time of my departure is at hand. I have fought a good fight, I have finished my course, I have kept the faith: henceforth there is laid up for me a crown of righteousness, which the Lord, the righteous judge, shall give me in that day: and not to me only, but unto all them also that love His appearing" (II Tim. 4:6-8).

EARLY CHRISTIAN PERSECUTION

The effect of Paul's preaching throughout parts of the Roman empire were earthshaking. It cut through all walks of life, affecting business, paganism, Judaism, slavery, and the Roman government itself. Turning to God from idols demanded a new loyalty to the risen Saviour, and followers of Christ became

309. Caesar — *"God and Saviour"*

310. *Colosseum at Rome*

most hated and despised. Accused of disloyalty to Rome and its gods, and in particular to the formalities of Caesar-worship, many were brutally beaten, imprisoned, and killed. What the Pharisees had once done to the church, now Rome was doing. At first, the persecution began as a social reaction, but developed into a political matter. Nero is regarded as the first persecutor when he used a small Christian community as a scapegoat for the burning of Rome.

A document has been discovered which reveals that homage was paid to Caesar as "God and Saviour" (*No. 309*), and a certificate (right), which shows that Roman citizens were obliged to affirm their allegiance to Caesar. They had to carry this certificate with them everywhere they went. Imagine a Christian being stopped by a Roman soldier to question him regarding his loyalty to Rome. If he could not produce a certificate to attest such loyalty, arrest was made. If testimony was made that Christ was indeed his Saviour, and he steadfastly refused to bow to the government's demands, he was sentenced to death. Paul's boldness before Festus and Agrippa is seen in this. Agrippa could have

interrupted Paul's testimony in Acts 26 anytime and demanded of him, as a Roman citizen, to produce evidence of his loyalty to Rome's Caesars. Paul's testimony was so interesting that God's Spirit, no doubt, blinded Agrippa's mind to this "point of order." *No. 310* shows the ruins of the old Roman Colosseum where it is believed many Christians were killed by wild beasts for their refusal to deny faith in *their* "God and Saviour, Jesus Christ." *No. 311* shows the ruins of the Colosseum's interior. The

311. *Colosseum Interior*

312. *Interior of a Catacomb*

313. *Catacomb Painting*

corridors and rooms located beneath the arena floor is where wild beasts, gladiators, and Christians were kept until they appeared before the spectators.

In our imagination of believers being stopped by Roman soldiers, we can see any number fleeing to the catacombs to escape arrest. Because of superstition, the soldiers would not enter these burial places; so Christians, if they managed to get inside, used such places to meet in secret for worship and fellowship. *No. 312* is the interior of one of the many New Testament catacombs. Roman Christians left paintings and inscribed symbols on the walls of these secret meeting places. *No. 313* is a catacomb painting, which depicts the testimony of these saints. The flowers speak of Christ's loveliness — the "Rose of Sharon," the "Lily of the field" — in the midst of Rome's ugliness. The doves speak of the inner witness of God's Spirit with theirs, and also of Christ's peace in their hearts in spite of Rome's persecution and tribulation (Rom. 8:16; John 16: 33).

No. 314 shows some of their symbols inside these gloomy catacombs. The "anchor" (left) indicated security in Christ. The letter "X" (right) in the Greek alphabet is "Chi" — the first letter in the name "Christ." The symbol of the sword with the "X" speaks of Christ, the "living Word." The "sign of the fish" (center) indicated a trust in "Jesus Christ, God's Son, Saviour." The initial letters in this Greek expression spell "icthus" — meaning "fish" (*No. 315*). This was the Christian's way of letting all Rome know that his trust was not in Caesar as "God and Saviour" (No. 309), but that his trust was in "Jesus Christ, God's Son, Saviour." In other words, "Caesars come and go, but our God lives forever!"

The Roman historian, Tacitus, who was not a Christian, records in his Annals the persecution of many Christians under Nero in A.D. 64, saying, "Nero . . . punished with the most ingenious cruelty, men whom the common people hated for their shameful crimes and called Christians. Christ, for whom the name was derived, had been put to death in the reign of Tiberius by the procurator Pontius Pilate. The deadly superstition, having been checked, began to break out again, not only throughout Judea, where this mischief first arose, but also at Rome, where from all sides all things scandalous and shameful meet and become fashion-

314. Christian Symbols

able. Therefore at the beginning some were seized who made confessions; then, on their information, a vast multitude was convicted, . . . [mainly due to their] hatred of the human race. And they were not only put to death, but subjected to insults, in that they were either made to dress up in the skins of wild beasts and perish by cruel mangling of dogs, or else put on crosses to be set on fire, and, as day declined, to be burned, being used as light by night. Nero had thrown open his garden for that spectacle, and gave a circus play, mingled with the people dressed in a charioteer's costume or driving in a chariot. From this arose toward men who were indeed criminals and deserving extreme penalties, sympathy, on the ground that they were destroyed not for the public good, but to satisfy the cruelty of an individual." No wonder Paul called Christ the "righteous Judge" (II Tim. 4:8). This was in contrast to Nero's rule and acts of atrocity.

Not too long after the Apostolic Age the faith of the Christians in Bithynia was. tested by Roman authorities under Trajan, as revealed in Pliny's letter to

315. Sign of the Fish

I = Jesus
X = Christ,
θ = God's
U = Son,
S = Saviour

204

Trajan in A.D. 112: "The method I have observed towards those who have been denounced to me as Christians is this: I interrogated them whether they were Christians; if they confessed it I repeated the question twice again, adding the threat of capital punishment; if they still persevered, I ordered their execution. Those who denied they were or had ever been Christians, who repeated after me an invocation to the gods, and offered adoration, with wine and frankincense, to your image, which I had ordered brought for that purpose, together with those of the gods, and who finally cursed Christ . . . , those I discharged."

While Rome sought to "stamp out" Christianity, their efforts only strengthened surviving believers. The "blood of the martyr became the seed of the church." The learned Jewish teacher, Gamaliel, had tried to warn the Jews of such dastardly actions against the church (Acts 5:29-39). It is no wonder the Saviour of all believers said concerning His church — "the gates of hell *shall not* prevail against it" (Matt. 16:18).

DESTRUCTION OF JERUSALEM, A.D. 70

When Christ foretold the destruction of Herod's Temple in Jerusalem, He clearly had in mind the destruction of the city itself (Luke 21:5, 6, 20-24). Because of Jewish rebellion against Rome's tyranny, armies were sent to and stationed in Palestine to keep order. During one such rebellion in A.D. 68, Vespasian's legionaires had routed the Jews in Jericho and destroyed the Essenes at Qumran (p. 165). Called back to Rome to become Emperor in A.D. 69, Vespasian was replaced by his son Titus, who fulfilled Christ's prophecy in A.D. 70 when he began the siege which brought about the destruction of Jerusalem. He ordered the city razed, the Temple destroyed, and was responsible for the slaughter of over 600,000 Jews. Thousands were taken captive. He celebrated

316. Spoils from Herod's Temple

his victory in Rome the following year, according to Josephus, accompanied by Jewish prisoners and the spoils of war, which included a copy of the Law, the golden table of showbread and the golden lampstand. He was made Emperor of Rome in A.D. 79, and died two years later. His Arch in Rome (*No. 316*), built to commemorate his victory over Jerusalem and dedicated after his death in A.D. 81, depicts his soldiers crowned with laurel and carrying the seven-branched lampstand, the table of show-bread, and the priests' trumpets from Herod's temple, which was standing in Christ's day.

Roman soldiers of the Tenth Legion were stationed by Titus in Jerusalem after its destruction to keep order. Many tiles bearing an inscription of this legion are excavated frequently, and some years ago a monument bearing this inscription, "Tenth Roman Legion," was discovered (*No. 317*). Further evidence of Jerusalem's destruction by Titus is seen on this

317. Tenth Roman Legion

318. Judaea-Capta Coin

"Judaea-Capta" coin (*No. 318*), which was minted to honor Titus. The reverse side shows two Jews in utter defeat, seated beneath a palm tree. The image of Titus is on the obverse side.

In many temples, stones were held together by gold or silver bars. The bars were bent and fitted into the holes and grooves, seen in this stone block (*No. 319*). The soldiers of Titus knew of this method of construction. They also knew

319. Temple Stone

that "to the victor belongs the spoils." To get to this precious metal, they literally took each stone from off top the other. The prediction of Christ regarding the destruction of the Temple could well have been brought about in this manner. He had said, "There shall not be left here one stone upon another" (Matt. 24: 1, 2).

The surviving Jews of Titus' fury were dispersed, many to Egypt and even to the uttermost parts of the earth (Deut. 28:64, 65). Some remained in the area. It is said that Jerusalem had no history for the next sixty years after its destruction. A Jewish leader named Bar Cochba sought to win freedom from the Romans about A.D. 134, but was overwhelmingly defeated by Hadrian, and what was left of Jerusalem was leveled to the ground — even foundations were plowed up. Two years later Rome began to build the city and all Jews were excluded from the area for the next two centuries, until the reign of Constantine. Just as it is impossible to rid the earth of the church, so it is impossible to exterminate God's chosen people, even though tried by a Pharaoh, the Assyrians, Nebuchadnezzar, Antiochus Epiphanes, Titus, Hadrian, Hitler, or the Arabs.

THE END OF THE NEW TESTAMENT ERA

John is the only New Testament author after the destruction of Jerusalem (unless, as some think, Jude wrote his Epistle). He wrote five books: the Fourth Gospel account, three Epistles, and the book of Revelation (or the Apocalypse). As though they are fighting God to the last, critics have waged one of their mightiest wars against the last author and books of the New Testament canon. Not only has John's authorship been questioned, but dates ascribed to his books also. At the end of the

nineteenth century radical critics placed the Gospel of John in the second Century A.D. Discovered in Egypt was a small piece of papyrus containing fragments of John 18:31-33, 37 and 38. Its style of writing was that of the first half of the second century — no later than A.D. 150. It was not only written in Egypt, but used there as well, and certainly points to the fact that the original book had been in circulation for some time *before* this copy was made.

The Revelation was written about A.D. 95 while John was on the isle of Patmos, banished there for his faith (Rev. 1:9). As early as about A.D. 250 Dionysius of Alexandria questioned its authorship because this book mentioned John's name and the Gospel account did not. The vocabulary and style of these two books have been questioned, which has led critics to say there were two different "John's." Late critics have contended Revelation was also written in the second century A.D. Archaeological findings show that definite historical references to the Apocalypse of John appear in the writings of Justine Martyr as early as A.D. 135, Irenaeus, in A.D. 180, who quoted Revelation five times and named John as the author, Clement of Alexandria, who received the book as authentic Scripture (A.D. 200), and the Muratorian Fragment, which lists it as part of the accepted New Testament canon (A.D. 170). These men certainly must have had copies of the original text of John long *after* he received it from the Lord.

John wrote to seven Churches of the Roman province of Asia, which is now a part of Turkey. There were other churches in this area, but these seem to have been selected because of different spiritual truths the Spirit sought to present to believers there and Christians in general. While archaeology can only provide a description of these cities as they were before and during John's day, their findings contribute to our understanding of expressions used by the author.

Some information has already been supplied on the city of *Ephesus* (p. 196). This is the first church John mentioned (Rev. 2:1-7). In Paul's day this city was vibrant, but when John wrote to its members, Ephesus was a dying city. Business was lagging and the Ephesians seemed to have lost the fire and creativeness and hope that made it a metropolis where one of the seven wonders of the ancient world was located. There seemed to be a resting now on the past. Christians in Ephesus had once been great. They were still true to what made them mature in Christ, but had lost their first love. How stinging John's words must have been as believers saw Ephesus dying naturally while they were dying spiritually!

When ancient writers made mention of *Smyrna* (Rev. 2:8-11), they referred to the "crown of Smyrna," which was probably a wreath of flowers worn by the followers of the goddess Cybele. The foundress of Smyrna in mythology was the Amazon Smyrna, who wore a high crown on her head. In John's day the city showed great faithfulness to Rome. With persecution still being carried out by the Romans, John's word of encouragement, "be thou faithful unto death, and I will give thee a crown of life" (vs. 10), could have had special significance. Later, in A.D. 155, Polycarp, a disciple of John, was martyred in Smyrna. He died saying: "Eighty and six years I have served him, and he hath done me no wrong. How can I speak evil of my King who saved me!" Polycarp was indeed "faithful unto death" in the city where his "spiritual father" had encouraged believers to stand for their faith.

Pergamos (Pergamum — Rev. 2:12-17) was the capital of the province. It was a religious center (or headquarters or "seat") for several cults. One was Roman Emperor worship. A temple for

320. Ephesus Today

this purpose had stood in this city since the time of Augustus in 29 B.C. Another god honored here was Asklepios, the god of healing, whose symbol was a serpent. This symbol has been found on some coins minted to honor this god. John, knowing the one back of all false religions — that old serpent, the devil — used the expression, "where Satan's seat is" (vs. 13), to encourage the Christians in Pergamos to remain true to Christ, and show no tolerance of these cults.

Thyatira (Rev. 2:18-29) was also noted for several cults, notably that of Apollos, the sun god and guardian deity of this city, and his father, Zeus, whose great altar was erected there. Trade guilds were a problem for Christians in the church. Ramsay found numerous inscriptions which mentioned workers of wool, linen, garments, dyes, leather, pottery, metal, and slave dealing. We are reminded immediately of "Lydia, a seller of purple, of the city of Thyatira" (Acts 16:14). Guild meetings with their banquets and merrymaking and intemperance posed a real threat to believers. John portrays Christ to them in contrast with Apollos, the incarnated son of Zeus — "The Son of God, who hath eyes like a flame, and his feet are like fine brass" (vs. 18), possibly to encourage them to keep their eyes on Him, and not on things round about.

Sardis (Rev. 3:1-6), a very large city, was in the center of numerous trade routes, and was formerly the capital of the rich kingdom of Lydia. The original city was practically impregnable, but because of neglect to keep watch, it was conquered by Cyrus of Persia in 564 B.C. In John's day, according to Roman historians, this city had a bad name for luxuriousness and revelry. John admonished believers to watch, lest they become involved in the ways of Sardis and the Lord overtake them like a thief in judgment (vs. 3).

Philadelphia (Rev. 3:7-13) was originally founded to spread Greek culture eastward. It was known as the "doorway" into Phrygia, the center of a wine industry, and various cults were entrenched among its people. John used the expression "open door" into Phrygia as an opportunity to remind believers there that God had given them an "open door" to spread the gospel to worshipers "in the synagogue of Satan" (vs. 9).

Laodicea (Rev. 3:14-22), like Philadelphia, was intended to be a "missionary" city to further Grecian culture, but because of its location at the crossroads in Asia Minor, it became guilty of commercial compromise. It became wealthy, and was known as a banking center. It was noted for its gloss black cloth, for a medical school, and for "Phrygian powder," a cure for weak eyes. They were so rich that when an earthquake destroyed their city and Rome offered assistance to rebuild, they refused and rebuilt the city themselves. Christians there had become guilty of material compromise and would well understand John's message regarding their spiritual blindness and poverty and nakedness. They knew the meaning of "white raiment" and "eyesalve" that would clothe them acceptably before God and would open the eyes of their spiritual understanding. John made them to understand they were in spiritual poverty, and that their money could not buy the things of God (vs. 18).

SUMMARY

From the beginning of our "expedition" in the first pages to our conclusion, there has been one thrill after another in supplementing the records of the Bible with "living messages" of a buried past — modern archaeological discoveries which have shed so much light on world history from God's point of view. When God employed the science of Archaeology, he gave to the champions of Scripture a new weapon to attack the "critics" of the Word — those who question the authenticity and trustworthiness of the fundamental doctrines of Christianity. Just as the "heavens declare the glory of God and the firmament showeth his handiwork," so the evidence, as shown in this volume, triumphantly confirms the authority of God's Holy Word. Today, it is the critic who is on the defensive and behind the times — not the Christian!

The greatest evidence that the Bible is the Word of God is the transformed life of one who has accepted its truths by faith, permitting the Holy Spirit to live the life of Christ within. Such a life no man can refute — like the blind man who said, "Once I was blind, now I see" (John 9:25). Though the believer accepts the Scriptures simply by faith, what a "spiritual shot in the arm" archaeological evidence has been in times like ours when unbelief is so popular. It has shown the critic that events recorded in the Bible actually happened, thus confirming its historical accuracy. It has further shown the critic that names of kings and nations mentioned in the Bible are not fictitious, that people mentioned *did indeed exist,* and that customs, so unfamiliar to us and appearing to be false, were in fact reality!

What has come to light thus far by the pick and spade of the archaeologist is by no means the end. It has whet the appetite to keep on digging — to excavate sites yet buried, to glean more information about God's Book, which has stood the tests of time.

THE ANVIL — GOD'S WORD

Last eve I paused beside a blacksmith's door,
  And heard the anvil ring the vesper chime;
Then looking in, I saw upon the floor,
  Old hammers, worn with beating years of time.
"How many anvils have you had," said I,
  "To wear and batter these hammers so?"
"Just one," said he, and then, with twinkling eye,
  "The anvil wears the hammers out, you know."

And so, thought I, the anvil of God's Word,
  For ages skeptic blows have beat upon;
Yet, though the noise of falling blows was heard,
  The anvil is unharmed — the hammers' gone.

And the Word of God *will* continue to stand the tests of time, no matter how many hammers future critics may wield! The believer can rest in God's promise, *"Truth shall spring out of the earth"* (Ps. 85:11). May God, then, help us to avoid the sins of Israel (I Cor. 10:5-11), adopt in principle the fourfold purpose of the Essene priests (p. 165), live as Christ lived (John 8:29), preach as Paul preached (II Cor. 1:19), contend for the faith like the early New Testament saints (Jude 3), and use all the evidence at our disposal to confirm the accuracy of God's Word — the Bible.

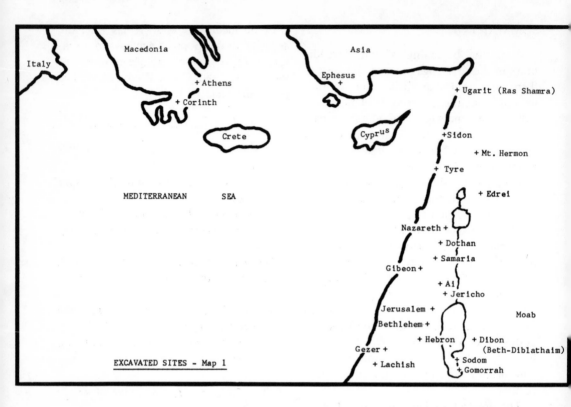

EXCAVATED SITES - Map 1

Italy

Macedonia

Asia

+ Athens

Ephesus +

+ Ugarit (Ras Shamra)

+ Corinth

+Sidon

+ Mt. Hermon

Crete

Cyprus

+ Tyre

MEDITERRANEAN   SEA

+ Edrei

Nazareth +

+ Dothan

+ Samaria

Gibeon +

+ Ai
+ Jericho

Jerusalem +

Moab

Bethlehem +

Gezer +

+ Hebron

+ Dibon
(Beth-Diblathaim)

+ Lachish

+ Sodom
+ Gomorrah

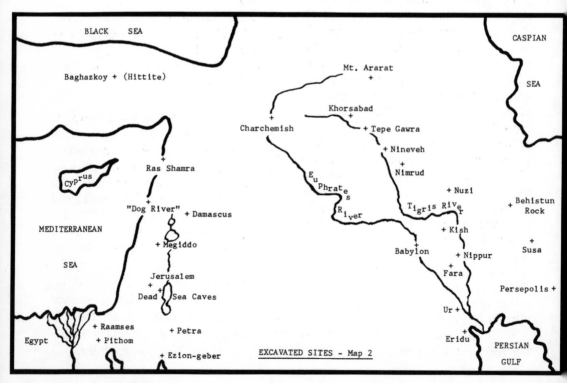

EXCAVATED SITES - Map 2

BLACK   SEA

CASPIAN

Baghazkoy + (Hittite)

Mt. Ararat
+

SEA

Khorsabad
+

Charchemish
+

+ Tepe Gawra

+ Nineveh

Ras Shamra
+

Cyprus

+ Nimrud

Euphrates
River

Tigris River

+ Nuzi

+ Behistun
Rock

"Dog River" + Damascus

MEDITERRANEAN

+ Kish

+ Megiddo

+ Susa

SEA

Babylon

+ Nippur

Jerusalem
+

+ Fara

Dead Sea Caves

Persepolis +

+ Raamses

Egypt

+ Pithom

+ Petra

Ur +

+ Ezion-geber

Eridu
+

PERSIAN

GULF

Bibliography

Albright, W. F., *The Archaeology of Palestine*, 1949, Penguin Books, Harmondsworth, Middlesex, England

Allegro, John M., *The People of the Dead Sea Scrolls*, 1958, Doubleday & Co., Garden City, N.Y.

Allis, O. T., "Israel and the Canaanites," Feb. 1, 1960, *Christianity Today*, Washington, D.C.

Blaiklock, E. M., *Out of the Earth*, 1957, Wm. B. Eerdmans, Grand Rapids, Mich.

Boyd, Bob, *Baal Worship in Old Testament Days*, 1966, Vernon Martin Associates, Lancaster, Penna.

Davis, John D., *A Dictionary of the Bible*, 1942, Baker Book House, Grand Rapids, Mich.

Free, Joseph P., *Archaeology and Bible History*, 1950, Van Kampen Press, Wheaton, Ill.

———, "Slight Variations in the Dead Sea Scrolls," April 14, 1956, *The Sunday School Times*, Philadelphia, Penna.

———, *Near Eastern Archaeology*, 1958, Vol. I, No. 4, Wheaton, Ill.

Garstang, John and J. B. E., *The Story of Jericho*, 1948, Marshall, Morgan & Scott, London, England

Gasque, W. Ward, *Sir William M. Ramsay*, 1966, Baker Book House, Grand Rapids, Mich.

Gordon, Maurice B., *Medicine Among the Ancient Hebrews*, 1941

Gurney, O. R., *The Hittites*, 1952, Penguin Books, Middlesex, England

Harris, R. L., "Archaeology and the Wilderness Tabernacle," Spring, 1964, *Near Eastern Archaeology*, Wheaton, Ill.

Keller, Werner, *The Bible as History*, 1958, William Morrow & Co., New York, N.Y.

Kelso, James L., "Archaeology's Role in Bible Study," July 22, 1957, *Christianity Today*, Washington, D.C.

Kinnaman, J. O., *Diggers for Facts*, 1940, Destiny Publishers, Haverhill, Mass.

Lance, H. Darrell, "Gezer in the Land and in History," May 1967, *The Biblical Archaeologist*, Cambridge, Mass.

Larue, Gerald A., "Prophets and Canaanites," June 6, 1960, *Christianity Today*, Washington, D.C.

LaSor, Wm. S., "The Dead Sea Scrolls after Twenty Years," Aug. 1, 1967, *The Sunday School Times and Gospel Herald*, Cleveland, O.

LeClant, Jean, *In the Steps of the Pharaohs*, 1958, Hasting Publishing House, New York, N.Y.

Miller, M. S. and J. L., *Encyclopedia of Bible Life*, 1944, Harper & Brothers, New York, N.Y.

National Geographic Magazine, Nov. 1901; Feb. 1944, Washington, D.C.

National Geographic Society, *Everyday Life in Ancient Times*, 1958, Washington, D. C.

Pfeiffer, Charles F., *Baker's Bible Atlas*, 1961, Baker Book House, Grand Rapids, Mich.

———, *Ras Shamra and the Bible*, 1962, Baker Book House, Grand Rapids, Mich.

———, *The Biblical World*, 1966, Baker Book House, Grand Rapids, Mich.

Price, Ira M., *The Monuments and the Old Testament*, 1958, Judson Press, Philadelphia, Penna.

Pritchard, James B., "Recent Discoveries in Gibeon," June 9, 1958, *Christianity Today*, Washington, D.C.

———, *The Ancient Near East in Pictures*, 1954, Princeton University Press, Princeton, N.J.

Rimmer, Harry, *Dead Men Tell Tales*, 1945, Wm. B. Eerdmans Publishing Co., Grand Rapids, Mich.

———, *Lot's Wife and the Science of Physics*, 1947, Eerdmans Publishing Co.

———, *The Harmony of Science and Scripture*, 1952, Eerdmans Publishing Co.

Shultz, Samuel J., *The Old Testament Speaks*, 1960, Harper & Row, Publishers, New York, N.Y.

Skehnan, P. W., "The Biblical Scrolls from Qumran and the Test of the Old Testament," September 1965, *The Biblical Archaeologist*

Steele, Francis R., "Archaeology and the Bible," Nov. 25, 1957, *Christianity Today*, Washington, D.C.

Stover, Gerald L., *Biblical Chronology*, 1966, Souderton, Penna.

Tenney, Merrill C., *Pictorial Bible Diction-*

211

ary, 1967, Zondervan Publishing House, Grand Rapids, Mich.

The Good News, 1953, American Bible Society, New York, N.Y.

Thompson, J. A., *The Bible and Archaeology,* 1962, Wm. B. Eerdmans Publishing Co., Grand Rapids, Mich.

Unger, Merrill F., *Unger's Bible Handbook,* 1966, Moody Press, Chicago, Ill.

Vos, Howard F., *An Introduction to Biblical Archaeology,* 1956, Moody Press, Chicago, Ill.

Wight, Fred H., *Highlights of Archaeology in Bible Lands,* 1955, Moody Press, Chicago, Ill.

Wiseman, D. J., *Illustrations from Biblical Archaeology,* 1958, Wm. B. Eerdmans Publishing Co., Grand Rapids, Mich.

Wiseman, P. J., *New Discoveries in Babylon about Genesis,* 1949, Marshall, Morgan & Scott, London, England

Woolley, Sir Leonard, *Ur of the Chaldees,* 1952, Penguin Books, Middlesex, England

Young, Edward J., "The Dead Sea Scrolls," Nov. 26, 1956, *Christianity Today,* Washington, D.C.

————, "The Dead Sea Scrolls and Christianity," June 1956, *His Magazine,* Chicago, Ill.

Illustration Credits

Index